SECOND EDITION

Functional Assessment and Program Development for Problem Behavior

A Practical Handbook

SECOND EDITION

Functional Assessment and Program Development for Problem Behavior

A Practical Handbook

Robert E. O'Neill
University of Utah

Robert H. Horner
University of Oregon

Richard W. Albin
University of Oregon

Jeffrey R. Sprague
University of Oregon

Keith Storey
Chapman University

J. Stephen Newton
University of Oregon

BROOKS/COLE
CENGAGE Learning

Australia • Brazil • Japan • Korea • Mexico • Singapore • Spain • United Kingdom • United States

BROOKS/COLE
CENGAGE Learning

Functional Assessment and Program Development for Problem Behavior: A Practical Handbook, Second Edition
Robert E. O'Neill, Robert H. Horner, Richard W. Albin, Jeffrey R. Sprague, Keith Storey, J. Stephen Newton

Sponsoring Editor: Vicki Knight

Marketing Team: Jean Vevers Thompson and Christine Davis

Editorial Assistant: Shelley Bouhaja

Production Editor: Laurel Jackson

Manuscript Editor: Patterson Lamb

Interior Design: Lisa Thompson

Cover Design: E. Kelly Shoemaker

Cover Photo: © Tony Freeman/PhotoEdit

Typesetting: Joan Mueller Cochrane

For product information and technology assistance, contact us at
Cengage Learning Customer & Sales Support, 1-800-354-9706

For permission to use material from this text or product, submit all requests online at **cengage.com/permissions**
Further permissions questions can be emailed to
permissionrequest@cengage.com

Library of Congress Cataloging-in-Publication Data

Functional assessment and program development for problem behavior : a practical handbook / Robert E. O'Neill ... [et al.]. — 2nd ed.
    p.   cm.
Rev. ed. of: Functional analysis of problem behavior.
Includes bibliographical references (p.).
ISBN-13: 978-0-534-26022-4
ISBN-10: 0-534-26022-5
    1. Behavioral assessment.   2. Handicapped—Functional assessment.
3. Behavior modification.   I. O'Neill, Robert E., [date]
II. Functional analysis of problem behavior.
RC473.B43F86   1997
616.89—dc20   96-41160
                                           CIP

Brooks/Cole
10 Davis Drive
Belmont, CA 94002-3098
USA

Cengage Learning is a leading provider of customized learning solutions with office locations around the globe, including Singapore, the United Kingdom, Australia, Mexico, Brazil, and Japan. Locate your local office at:
international.cengage.com/region

Cengage Learning products are represented in Canada by Nelson Education, Ltd.

For your course and learning solutions, visit **academic.cengage.com**

Purchase any of our products at your local college store or at our preferred online store **www.ichapters.com**

Printed in the United States of America
21 22 23 24 14 13 12 11

To the children and adults with disabilities who taught us how to conduct and use functional assessment procedures; and to the families, teachers, and community staff who used early drafts of the tools in this book and helped us understand how to make these tools more practical and effective

ABOUT THE AUTHORS

ROBERT E. O'NEILL is an associate professor in the Department of Special Education at the University of Utah. He has been involved in direct service, research, training, and model development activities relating to persons with disabilities since 1978. After receiving his M.S. and Ph.D. from the University of California at Santa Barbara, Dr. O'Neill was a member of the faculty of the University of Oregon for nine years. His research and teaching interests focus on strategies for supporting persons with disabilities and severe problem behaviors in typical school, work, and other community settings. His work has focused in the areas of functional assessment, teaching communication skills as alternatives to problem behaviors, and systems for teacher collaboration and support in school settings. He has published over 30 articles, books, and book chapters and has made presentations at a variety of state, national, and international conferences. Dr. O'Neill's work has appeared in the *Journal of Applied Behavior Analysis, Journal of the Association for Persons with Severe Handicaps, Education and Treatment of Children, Journal of Developmental and Physical Disabilities, Journal of Special Education,* and *Remedial and Special Education.*

ROBERT H. HORNER is a professor of education at the University of Oregon, Director of the Specialized Training Program, head of the Department of Special Education and Community Resources, and the Oregon *UAP* Technical Assistance Coordinator. He has a 20-year professional history of direct service, research, program development, and training in the field of severe disabilities. Dr. Horner has directed numerous federal research, demonstration, and personnel preparation projects. Many of these projects involved activities and topic areas related to research and development work on residential support and employment for persons with severe disabilities, instructional and behavioral support technology, and personnel training and staff development.

For the past six years, Dr. Horner has served as Project Director for the Rehabilitation Research and Training Center on Positive Behavioral Support, a six-university collaboration that has played a leading role in research, training, and dissemination on positive behavioral support technology. Dr. Horner is currently an associate editor for the *American Journal on Mental Retardation* and is a past editor of the *Journal of Applied Behavior Analysis* and the *Journal of the Association for Persons with Severe Handicaps*. Dr. Horner has been actively involved in preservice and inservice training for teachers and adult service personnel since 1977.

RICHARD W. ALBIN is a senior research associate/associate professor in the Department of Special Education and Community Resources at the University of Oregon. For the past 16 years, Dr. Albin has worked within the Specialized Training Program at the University of Oregon on a variety of research, training, and model development projects that are focused on providing support for people with moderate and severe intellectual disabilities in school and community settings. Dr. Albin has written or co-written numerous papers and book chapters related to teaching procedures for learners with intellectual disabilities; positive behavioral support procedures in school, home, and community settings; and development of inservice and staff training systems and materials. He has collaborated in providing training and ongoing support and technical assistance for a national network of state training teams in positive behavioral support procedures.

JEFFREY R. SPRAGUE has over 20 years' experience as a classroom teacher, teacher supervisor, consultant, researcher, and teacher of methodological issues related to special education services for persons with disabilities. Dr. Sprague spent seven years as a model-classroom teacher (Arc of Lane County and Oregon Teacher of the Year) for the Oregon High School Project for Secondary Age Students with Disabilities. He collaborated with Dr. Barbara Wilcox and Dr. Thomas Bellamy to develop and test inclusive, community-based school and work services and classroom management technologies. Dr. Sprague also served as a behavior management consultant and trainer in the Lane Educational Service District Program for Students with Severe Disabilities. He has extensive experience in supporting teacher trainees, direct-care staff in vocational and residential settings, and families. He is the author of several widely used manuals and book chapters on integration and peer involvement systems for school-age children. As director of the Indiana University Center for School and Community Integration, he directed the OSEP-funded Statewide Transition Systems Change Project; the Severe Disabilities Statewide Systems Change Project for school inclusion; and the *Peer Education Project,* which developed a curriculum for high school students to learn important concepts related to disability. Dr. Sprague also directed a project entitled *Multi-Variable Analysis of Severe Problem Behavior,*

which focused on identifying complex antecedent variables that affect problem behavior.

Dr. Sprague is an assistant professor at the Specialized Training Program and the Associate Director of the University of Oregon Institute on Violence and Destructive Behavior. His activities include research; model development; field-based technical assistance; development and implementation of local, state, and national training events; and product development and dissemination. Dr. Sprague is recognized in Oregon and across the nation as a leader in positive behavioral support and in promoting systems change related to secondary and school-to-work issues.

KEITH STOREY is currently an assistant professor in the Department of Education at Chapman University in Concord, California. He served six years as a classroom teacher working with people with a variety of disability labels. He received his Ph.D. in 1989 at the University of Oregon. Dr. Storey is the recipient of the 1988 Alice H. Hayden Award from The Association for Persons with Severe Handicaps and of the 1996 Hau-Cheng Wang Fellowship from Chapman University, which is presented for exceptional merit in scholarship.

J. STEPHEN NEWTON is the coordinator of the Neighborhood Living Project at the University of Oregon's Specialized Training Program. He received his B.A. in psychology from the University of North Carolina at Chapel Hill in 1970 and his M.S. and Ph.D. in special education/developmental disabilities from the University of Oregon in 1986 and 1991. His research interests include outcome systems for residential services and social support for people with severe disabilities.

C O N T E N T S

CHAPTER ONE
Introduction   1

Purpose of the Handbook 1
Who Should Use This Handbook? 2
Functional Assessment 3
What Is a Functional Assessment? 3
An Overview of Three Approaches for Functional Assessment 4
  Informant Methods 4
  Direct Observation 5
  Functional Analysis 6
Why Conduct a Functional Assessment? 6
Before Conducting a Functional Assessment: Additional Issues to Consider 7
  Person-Centered Planning 7
  Activity Patterns and Social Life 7
  Medical and Physical Issues 7
A Statement of Values 8

CHAPTER TWO
Functional Assessment and Analysis Strategies   9

The Functional Assessment Interview (FAI) 9
  Who Should Be Interviewed? 9
  What Are the Outcomes of a Functional Assessment Interview? 10
  How Long Does the Interview Take? 10
  Using the Functional Assessment Interview (FAI) Form 10
  Developing Summary Statements 16
Including the Individual: The Student-Directed Functional
  Assessment Interview 17

Who Should Be Interviewed? 17
Who Should Conduct the Student-Directed Interview? 27
How Long Does the Interview Take? 27
What Are the Outcomes of a Student-Directed Interview? 27
Using the Student-Directed Functional Assessment Interview Form 27
Validating the Student-Directed Functional Assessment Interview 35
Direct Observation 35
Keep It Simple 35
When and Where Should Observations Be Done? 36
Who Should Observe? 36
How Long Should Direct Observation Data Be Collected? 36
What Does the Functional Assessment Observation Form Do? 37
The Content of the Functional Assessment Observation Form 37
Using the Functional Assessment Observation Form 42
Exercise in Form Setup, Observation, and Recording 44
Interpreting Functional Analysis Observation Form Data 46
Confirming or Revising Initial Summary Statements 47
Examples in Analyzing Data from Direct Observations 48
Decision Making Based on Observational Data 53
Functional Analysis Manipulations 54
When Should Functional Analysis Be Done? 55
Who Should Be Involved? 55
The Process of Conducting a Functional Analysis 55
Ideas for Testing Different Types of Summary Statements 57
Examples of Functional Analysis Manipulations 58
Important Considerations and Guidelines Concerning
Functional Analysis Procedures 61

CHAPTER THREE
Building Behavior Support Plans

65

Four Considerations for Building Behavior Support Plans 65
Behavior Support Plans Describe *Our* Behavior 65
Behavior Support Plans Should Build from Functional Assessment Results 66
Behavior Support Plans Should Be Technically Sound 66
Behavior Support Plans Should "Fit" the Setting
Where They Will Be Implemented 68
Selecting Intervention Procedures: The Competing Behavior Model 69
Constructing a Competing Behavior Model 69
Competing Behavior Model for Erica 76
Competing Behavior Model for Cornell 78
Competing Behavior Model for Stewart 78
Competing Behavior Model for Curtis 78

CHAPTER FOUR
Writing Behavior Support Plans

85

Why Write Behavior Support Plans? 85
Elements of Behavior Support Plans 85
    Operational Descriptions 86
    Summary Statements 86
    General Approach 86
    Key Routines 86
    Monitoring and Evaluation 87
    Example Behavior Support Plan: Mara 87

Conclusion

91

Appendixes

A: List of References Relevant to Functional Assessment 93
B: Functional Assessment Interview Form (FAI) 99
C: Student-Directed Functional Assessment Interview Form 109
D: Blank Functional Assessment Observation Form 115
E: Functional Assessment Observation Form for Yolanda 117
F: Summary Statements for Observation Form Examples 119
G: Blank Competing Behavior Model Form 121

FIGURES

2.1   Defining the Consequences That Maintain Problem Behaviors 13

2.2   Completed Functional Assessment Interview (FAI) for Curtis Jackson 18

2.3   Example of Completed Daily Schedule Matrix 29

2.4   Summary Diagram of Problem Behavior Situation 30

2.5   Completed Example of the Student-Directed Functional Assessment Interview 31

2.6   Functional Assessment Observation Form 38

2.7   Completed Observation Form for Joe 41

2.8   Blank Observation Form for Exercise 45

2.9   Completed Observation Form for Erin 49

2.10 Completed Observation Form for Peter 51

2.11 Completed Observation Form for Curtis 52

2.12 Functional Analysis Manipulation of Antecedent Conditions
      (Easy Versus Hard Tasks) for Greg 59

2.13 Functional Analysis Manipulation of Consequence Conditions for Ben 60

2.14 An Example of Brief Functional Assessment with Shante 62

3.1   Your Diagram of a Summary Statement 71

3.2   Expanded Competing Behavior Model 71

3.3   Derrick's Expanded Competing Behavior Model 72

3.4   Mara's Assessment Information 72

3.5   Competing Behavior Diagram for Mara 73

3.6   Competing Behavior Model for Marlene 74

3.7   Competing Behavior Model Form 75

3.8   Competing Behavior Model and Intervention Strategies for Mara 77

3.9   Competing Behavior Model and Intervention Strategies for Erica 79

3.10 Competing Behavior Model and Intervention Strategies for Cornell 80

3.11 Competing Behavior Model and Intervention Strategies for Stewart 81

3.12 Competing Behavior Model for Curtis: Yelling and Throwing 82

3.13 Competing Behavior Model for Curtis: Pinching and Scratching 83

3.14 Competing Behavior Model for Curtis: Calling Out, Slapping, and Pounding 84

4.1 Behavior Support Plan for Mara 88

BOXES

1.1 The Five Primary Outcomes of the Functional Assessment Process 3

1.2 Three Strategies for Collecting Functional Assessment Information 4

2.1 Examples of Summary Statements Based on Interview Information 17

2.2 Steps for Setting Up a Functional Assessment Observation Form for Collecting Data 40

2.3 Basic Steps for Recording Data on the Functional Assessment Observation Form 43

2.4 Basic Guidelines for Interpreting Data from the Functional
Assessment Observation Form 48

2.5 Guidelines for Conducting Functional Analysis Manipulations 64

3.1 The Three Steps Involved in Completing a Competing Behavior Model 69

PREFACE

The development of the second edition of this handbook was prompted by a number of issues. Substantial conceptual and technological advances continue to be made in approaches for analyzing patterns of problem behavior and developing support programs, and we wanted to incorporate them into the handbook. Also, we have modified the forms and procedures in the first edition in ways we believe will improve both the efficiency and effectiveness of the functional assessment process. Above all, we were strongly motivated to continue providing teachers, clinicians, and family members with practical strategies to help them in their daily work.

The majority of this handbook is devoted to strategies that are considered part of functional assessment rather than functional analysis. Functional assessment is a broad process for gathering information to understand problem behavior situations and develop effective support plans. Functional analysis is a process for conducting experimental analyses of the contingencies that maintain problem behaviors. The definitions of these terms and the strategies involved in both approaches are discussed in detail in a number of sections of the handbook.

To make the handbook easy to read, we have purposely avoided providing a large number of references in the text. Instead, we have provided a list of references and resources relevant to functional assessment and analysis in Appendix A. Readers interested in relevant research and other related material should consult this list.

Efforts to support persons who exhibit serious problem behaviors will always involve some level of risk to the person themselves and to the staff and family members attempting to support them. We have made every effort to recommend appropriate safety guidelines throughout this handbook. However, we recognize that no procedures can absolutely guarantee the safety of people involved in problematic situations. Therefore, we must declare that all responsibility for ensuring the safety of individuals who become involved in procedures described in this handbook lies with those implementing and supervising the procedures (such as teachers, psychologists, parents and family members, residential and vocational staff, and consultants). No legal responsibility or obligation for personal safety is accepted by the United States government; the University of Oregon; the University of Utah; Chapman University; the states of Oregon, Utah, and California; the authors of this manual; or the publisher.

Acknowledgments

We acknowledge the many teachers, family members, consultants, researchers, and others who have implemented the strategies described in the first edition of this book and who have provided feedback on both positive features and aspects that would benefit from revision. In particular, we thank Drs. Edward Carr, Glen Dunlap, Wayne Sailor, Lynn Koegel, Robert Koegel, Daniel Baker, and Jacki Anderson for their helpful input and feedback in the preparation of this second edition. Appreciation also is extended to Patty Bennett and Wendy Weller for their technical contributions in the preparation of the

manuscript. We also acknowledge our significant debt to the children and adults with disabilities who have provided guidance and feedback in the design and revision of procedures described here.

Robert E. O'Neill
Robert W. Horner
Richard W. Albin
Jeffrey R. Sprague
Keith Storey
J. Stephen Newton

CHAPTER ONE

Introduction

Purpose of the Handbook

This handbook presents specific forms and procedures for the functional assessment of problem behaviors and for the use of this information in developing comprehensive behavioral support plans. Functional assessment is the general label used to describe a set of processes for defining the events in an environment that reliably predict and maintain problem behaviors. Functional assessment can include interviews, rating scales, direct observations, and systematic, experimental analysis of problem situations. These experimental analyses, in which behavior is observed while elements of the environment are manipulated (in such ways as giving rewards following problem behavior), are a part of functional assessment and carry the label *functional analysis*. Over the past decade, major effort has been focused on identifying the simplest and most efficient strategies for conducting functional assessments and analyses. More recently, attention has turned to procedures for using functional assessment and analysis information to design effective behavioral support strategies. The procedures presented in this handbook represent outcomes of that effort.

The purpose of this handbook is to present the logic, forms, and examples that will allow the reader to (a) conduct a functional assessment in typical school, work, or community settings, and (b) develop a behavioral support plan that addresses problem behaviors.

We have prepared this handbook because we believe that the opportunities for people with severe problem behavior to experience a high quality of life as regular members of school, work, and community settings are dependent on our ability to collaborate with them in designing effective support. Problem behaviors are a barrier to community life only if adequate support is not available.

This handbook presents a basic approach to functional assessment and program design as well as *specific* forms and procedures that have proven useful in schools, work settings, and homes. When used properly, these materials and procedures can contribute significantly to effective behavioral support for individuals in our communities.

We have developed this handbook with appreciation for changes that are occurring in the field of behavioral support. One important development is recognition that effective behavioral support should not only help to reduce problem behaviors but should also change the opportunities a person has for learning new skills, for social inclusion, for access to meaningful activities, and for basic participation in the local community. Behavioral support is effective when it positively affects how a person lives as well as reduces the dangers imposed by problem behaviors.

A second major change in behavioral support is emphasis on comprehensive interventions. These typically involve multiple components. Comprehensive interventions focus not only on the consequences for appropriate and problem behaviors but also on the redesign of those antecedent conditions that predict problem behaviors: medical issues, architectural issues, curricular issues. In addition, comprehensive interventions are aimed not just at reducing problem behaviors but also at teaching individuals new skills that make problem behaviors less likely.

Functional assessment is a process of understanding the physiological and environmental factors that contribute to a person's problem behaviors. The whole purpose of a functional assessment is to gain information that will improve the effectiveness and efficiency of behavioral interventions. As our vision of behavioral interventions has expanded, so has the need to modify assessment procedures. Understanding the consequences that maintain problem behaviors, for example, is an essential element of a functional assessment. But if the information from the assessment is intended to help people redesign the physical context of a living setting, the curriculum in a school, or the social structure in a work environment, the assessment must also provide details about the physical and social environment that sets the occasion for problem behaviors.

Functional assessment is not like a medical diagnosis. The information from a functional assessment does *not* allow a simple match of a problem behavior with a prepackaged clinical intervention. Functional assessment is a process for redesigning environments so they "work" for people with communication and behavioral disabilities. It is an "intimate" process. It requires the collaborative participation of the person with disabilities, those who know that person best, and often a person with significant competence in the theory and procedures of behavior analysis. Together this team can use the information from the functional assessment to craft a system of support that melds medical, architectural, behavioral, and educational variables to create effective environments. Our hope is that the procedures in this handbook will help in the design of schools, homes, communities, and workplaces for people who have histories of problem behavior.

Who Should Use This Handbook?

The handbook is designed to assist a variety of people who have or share the responsibility for building plans and providing behavioral support for people with problem behaviors. The procedures and forms that we describe have been useful for teachers (regular and special education), school counselors, school psychologists, support staff for adults in work and residential settings, and family members involved in supporting another family member. Our particular intent is to provide tools that will help professionals and others working with people who present severe, complex, problem behaviors. These behaviors often do not respond to simple support strategies and require more than casual observation to understand. The tools in this handbook should be helpful in defining effective strategies for supporting these individuals.

Problem behaviors may take many forms, such as self-injurious hits and bites, violent and aggressive attacks, destruction of property, and other seriously disruptive behaviors (such as screaming or tantrums). The individuals who exhibit problem behaviors may be labeled in a variety of ways—developmentally disabled, autistic, mentally retarded, mentally ill, emotionally or behaviorally disordered (EBD), severely emotionally disturbed (SED), having traumatic brain injury—or they may carry no formal diagnostic labels. These individuals may vary greatly in terms of their overall support needs and ability to communicate and participate in their own behavioral support. The functional assessment procedures and forms described in this handbook can be used in addressing the behavioral support needs of people exhibiting the full range of problem behaviors and labels encountered in school, work, residential, and other community settings.

We encourage you to modify and adapt the tools in this handbook. Depending on your professional role or on the particular situation or circumstances that you encounter, you may find minor variations of our forms and procedures useful. We have designed the forms and procedures to be flexible. Please copy, revise, and modify these forms in any manner that is useful for your own situations.

This handbook is designed to serve as a *guide* to functional assessment and program development processes. It does not present comprehensive information on a wide range of behavioral support strategies. The tools presented have been found to assist competent people to be more effective, but they are not described in the detail needed for people just beginning in the field. We assume that users of this handbook will have basic training and experience in the theory and tactics of applied behavior analysis. For more in-depth discussion of the theory, research basis, and intervention procedures associated with applied behavior analysis, please refer to the references listed in Appendix A.

Functional Assessment

Problem behaviors often are a source of confusion and frustration. The person engaging in problem behaviors may appear to find the behavior difficult and painful. The families, teachers, support staff, and advocates of the person frequently are confused and distressed over the challenge of trying to alter such behavior patterns. In many situations, problem behaviors may not only be dangerous but may also seem inexplicable. Such patterns of behavior do not fit with the way we think the world should work and often don't make sense to people in the throes of the dilemma created by their occurrence. One of the goals of a good functional assessment is to bring clarity and understanding to otherwise chaotic and confusing situations. We seldom reach this goal by focusing on diagnostic labels (such as autism, mental retardation, Down syndrome) or the simple topography or form of the problem behavior (such as hitting, kicking, screaming). Order is achieved through a systematic assessment and understanding of the variables that set the occasion for the occurrence (or nonoccurrence) of problem behaviors and the consequences that maintain those behaviors.

What Is a Functional Assessment?

Functional assessment is a process for gathering information that can be used to maximize the effectiveness and efficiency of behavioral support. A functional assessment is complete when five main outcomes have been achieved, as shown in Box 1.1.

BOX 1.1 The Five Primary Outcomes of the Functional Assessment Process

1. A clear *description of the problem behaviors,* including classes or sequences of behaviors that frequently occur together
2. Identification of the events, times, and situations that *predict* when the problem behaviors *will* and *will not* occur across the full range of typical daily routines
3. Identification of the *consequences that maintain the problem behaviors* (that is, what functions the behaviors appear to serve for the person)
4. Development of one or more *summary statements* or hypotheses that describe specific behaviors, a specific type of situation in which they occur, and the outcomes or reinforcers maintaining them in that situation
5. Collection of *direct observation data* that support the summary statements that have been developed

The processes used in conducting a functional assessment can take many forms and have many levels of precision. Anyone who has ever used an A-B-C (Antecedent-Behavior-Consequence) chart has conducted one form of functional assessment. Anyone who has observed undesirable behavior in different situations and concluded that "she does that because . . ." or "he does that in order to . . ." has developed a type of summary statement concerning variables influencing behavior. Our experience has been that a functional assessment is helpful in the design of behavioral support once the assessment information allows confident prediction of the conditions in which the problem behavior is likely to occur and not occur, and when there is agreement about the consequences that appear to maintain the problem behavior. Recently, several researchers and experienced clinicians have begun advocating functional assessment procedures in which the intensity of the assessment matches the complexity of the problem behavior. That is, if less rigorous and easy to implement assessment procedures produce a confident description of the events that predict and maintain a problem behavior, there is no reason to use more rigorous and precise procedures. If, however, a procedure such as an interview does not generate clear and compelling patterns, then more intense and precise observations and manipulations may be warranted. The procedures and tools described in this handbook offer a range of efficient strategies for conducting a comprehensive functional assessment. In fact, in their entirety, the procedures presented here may be more comprehensive than a clinician or practitioner (behavior specialist, teacher, program manager) often needs for the design of a typical support plan. However, the full range of assessment approaches and options needed for those individuals and situations in which a durable and complex behavior, or group of behaviors, has been identified is included.

An Overview of Three Approaches for Functional Assessment

Specific methods for collecting functional assessment information fall into three general strategies: informant methods, direct observation, and functional analysis (Box 1.2).

Informant Methods

The first strategy for conducting functional assessment is to talk to the person with problem behaviors (if possible) and to those people who have direct contact with and knowledge about the individual. You may have had occasion to provide information about the occurrence of problem behaviors or to seek such information from relevant others (parents, teachers). Interviews (even self-interviews) and other informant methods (questionnaires, rating scales) can be useful in defining and narrowing the range of variables that may affect the behaviors of concern. Interviews also are typically a good way of pulling

---

BOX 1.2 Three Strategies for Collecting Functional Assessment Information

Strategy 1: Informant methods. Talk to the individual and/or to those who know the individual best.

Strategy 2: Direct observation. Observe the person in natural conditions over an extended time period.

Strategy 3: Functional analysis manipulations. Systematically manipulate potential controlling variables (consequences or structural variables) in analog or natural conditions and observe effects on the person's behavior.

together the body of existing knowledge regarding a person's patterns of behavior.

A major goal of any interview procedure is to identify which of the hundreds of events in an environment seem to be linked to the specific problem behavior of a specific person. When you are conducting an interview, consider the daily routines the person performs. If you are focusing on a child in school, what are the routines of the classroom? How do children enter the room? What are the morning activities? What happens during transitions? How do children move from room to room? What happens during recess and lunch? Consider the problem behaviors in the context of the established routines. Use the interview questions to understand what features of these routines appear salient for the person. What changes in these features seem to be associated with increases and decreases in problem behavior? Two individuals in the same setting with the same diagnosis and the same type of problem behavior may be responding to extremely different features. One goal of the interview is to understand which of the many antecedent and consequence features in that setting and routine are associated with the problem behaviors.

Remember that part of a good functional assessment is to place the problem behavior in a context. Too often we talk and operate as if people "have" behaviors. Behavior analysis has taught us that we should always talk about behavior as occurring in contexts, not in people. Fredda is not a biter; rather, when presented with food she does not like, Fredda will bite her wrist until the undesired food is removed. If we consider problem behaviors as occurring in people, it is logical to try to change the people. If we consider problem behaviors as occurring in contexts, it becomes logical to change the context. Behavior change occurs by changing environments, not trying to change people. Functional assessment is a process for understanding the context (antecedents and consequences) associated with problem behaviors. Interviews are one valuable tool for identifying the features of a context that are important for or associated with a person's problem behavior.

Many examples of functional assessment interviews and questionnaires can be found in the literature. In most cases, however, they share an emphasis on gaining information about the following:

1. What are the problem behaviors that are causing concern?
2. What events or physical conditions that occur significantly earlier in time prior to the problem behavior increase the predictability that the problem behavior will occur?
3. What events and situations that occur just prior to the problem behaviors reliably predict occurrence of problem behaviors? What events reliably predict that problem behaviors will *not* occur?
4. Given a specific situation when the problem behavior occurs, what are the consequences that appear to maintain the problem behavior?
5. What appropriate behaviors (if any) could produce the same consequences that appear to maintain the problem behavior?
6. What can we learn from previous behavior support efforts about strategies that are ineffective, partially effective, or effective for only a short time?

Direct Observation

The second strategy for collecting functional assessment information is to systematically observe the person with problem behavior in typical daily routines. Systematic, direct observation has long been the foundation of applied use of behavioral procedures. In the 1960s, Dr. Sidney Bijou and his colleagues provided the first strategies for using this approach to get assessment information. Direct observations usually are done by teachers, direct support staff, and/or family members who already work or live with the person. The observations must be done in a manner that does not interfere with normal daily events or require extensive training. In most cases, the observers record when a problem behavior occurs, what was happening just before the behavior, what happened after the behavior, and their perception of the function of the behavior in that instance. When such information is collected for 10 to 15 instances of the problem behavior, it typically allows observers an opportunity to discover whether a pattern exists that will allow determination of the following:

1. What problem behaviors happen together?
2. When, where, and with whom are problem behaviors most likely?
3. What consequences appear to maintain occurrence of the problem behavior?

In Chapter 2, we present a Functional Assessment Observation Form. We have found this form to be practical, efficient, and effective for confirming and building on information obtained from more indirect informant methods.

Functional Analysis

The third strategy for gathering functional assessment information involves the systematic manipulation of specific variables that are or are not associated with the problem behaviors. In conducting a functional analysis, you systematically monitor behavior while manipulating the environment. One frequently used method of functional analysis involves the manipulation of consequences contingent on the occurrence of targeted behaviors. Another method involves manipulating structural variables such as task difficulty, task length, level of attention provided during an activity, or the presence or absence of choice in an activity. Functional analysis amounts to a formal test of the relationship between environmental variables and the occurrence or nonoccurrence of problem behaviors. Functional analysis is the most precise, rigorous, and controlled method of conducting a functional assessment. Functional analysis is the only approach that allows unambiguous demonstration of a functional relationship between environmental events and problem behaviors. Brian Iwata and his colleagues have pioneered a powerful approach to functional analysis, and

this approach has been adapted by F. C. Mace, David Wacker, Timothy Vollmer, and others. Functional analysis can be expensive in time and energy, but in some cases, it may be the only way to ensure an adequate assessment of problem behaviors. Because functional analysis involves creating situations that will provoke the problem behavior and because success of the process requires research-like skills, it is seldom wise for a functional analysis to be conducted without the direct involvement of a person trained in conducting behavior-analytic research.

This handbook presents specific procedures for implementing each of these three functional assessment strategies. Our emphasis, however, will be on interview and direct observation methods because we believe these are the most applicable in typical homes, schools, and communities. The key issue to remember is that these strategies are designed to identify the relationships between problem behaviors and the antecedents and consequences that occasion and maintain these behaviors. The assumption is that by understanding these relationships we can develop plans of behavioral support that (a) will be more effective, (b) will be more efficient, and (c) will produce broader change in the lifestyle of the individual with problem behaviors.

Why Conduct a Functional Assessment?

There are two central reasons for conducting a functional assessment. The first is that information about when, where, and why problem behaviors occur is extremely valuable in building effective and efficient behavioral support. If interventions are developed without a functional assessment, they may make problem behaviors worse. We have all seen instances in which a child was having tantrums to gain a treat and then was told she could have the treat if she were quiet, or a child who was behaving aggressively to avoid a task and was sent to the corner for her behavior. In each case, the presumed solution actually reinforced the problem behavior. The danger of making problem behaviors worse is very real. Functional assessment not only helps in the development of effective and efficient plans, but it also helps us avoid programmatic errors.

The second reason a functional assessment should be done with severe problem behaviors is that it is now a professional standard. The Association for Behavior Analysts published a "Right to Effective Treatment" (Van Houten et al., 1988), which includes the right of all individuals who receive behavioral intervention to a professionally competent functional assessment. The National Institutes of Health conducted an important consensus conference on dangerous and destructive behavior (NIH Consensus Report, 1989) which strongly endorsed the use of functional assessment procedures. More recently, a number of states (Minnesota, Florida, California, Utah, Washington, Oregon, New York) have instituted laws or state regulations stipulating the need for a functional assessment prior to significant behavioral interventions.

Functional assessment is now a professional standard for psychologists, teachers, and adult service providers delivering behavioral support to children and adults with disabilities. The use of functional assessment not only makes programmatic sense; it is an expected practice in the field.

Before Conducting a Functional Assesment: Additional Issues to Consider

Given the need for a broad impact, behavioral support can often benefit from companion assessment procedures. Three companion sources of assessment data that we have used include (a) person-centered planning, (b) activity pattern assessment, and (c) assessment of medical/physical issues.

Person-Centered Planning

During the last ten years, a variety of approaches have been developed to create a per-

son-centered plan, or vision of the future for an individual. This plan is developed with all the individuals actively involved in a person's life. Typically, there is a broad focus, including the personal preferences and strengths of the person and not just the problems and difficulties he or she experiences. The process of personal futures planning offers a broader context in which to build behavior support plans. It is through this broader process that we follow the advice of the noted behavior analyst Dr. Todd Risley to begin good behavioral support by helping a person "get a life" and then build in the more detailed behavior support systems that may be needed.

Activity Patterns and Social Life

Our quality of life, and therefore our behavior, is greatly influenced by the activities in which we engage and the social life we experience. In analyzing people's activity patterns, you can address issues such as the variety of activities they perform, the degree of community integration they experience, and the extent to which their preferences are reflected and accommodated. In considering their social life, the makeup of their social network (size, presence or absence of significant others, longevity of relationships) and the nature of their social interactions (such as number of opportunities to engage in preferred activities with preferred people) can provide important clues to the changes needed in support. Two instruments referenced in Appendix A, the Resident Lifestyle Inventory (Kennedy, Horner, Newton, & Kanda, 1990) and the Social Network Analysis Form (Kennedy, Horner, & Newton, 1990) have proven useful in analyzing these lifestyle issues. We recommend their inclusion or the use of similar instruments within the comprehensive assessment process leading to a behavioral support plan.

Medical and Physical Issues

Dr. Jon Bailey has emphasized the need to examine medical or physical conditions that may be influencing problem behaviors. Too often behavioral interventions have been used to address problem behaviors that have a medical etiology. One important concern is to identify or rule out the presence of low-incidence syndromes that are associated with specific patterns of severe problem behaviors. Also, many conditions including allergies, sinus or middle ear infections, premenstrual and menstrual cycle effects, urinary tract infections, toothaches, and chronic constipation may exacerbate the occurrence of particular behaviors. The effects and side effects of medication regimes represent a major area often requiring attention, given the large number of persons with disabilities who receive a variety of neuroleptic, seizure control, and other types of medications. Determining the influence of such medical/physical variables and developing strategies for dealing with them typically require a collaborative support process that includes appropriate medical personnel to provide the necessary services.

A Statement of Values

Functional assessment is not a value-free technology. We offer the materials and procedures in this handbook with three value-based assumptions. *The first is that behavioral support must be conducted with the dignity of the person as a primary concern.* Functional assessment is appropriate because it acknowledges that a person's behavior is functional. People do not engage in self-injury, aggression, severe property destruction, or seriously disruptive behaviors solely because they have mental retardation or other developmental disabilities. Rather, they engage in patterns of behavior that have worked for them and continue to work for them in some way. There is a logic to their

behavior, and functional assessment is an attempt to understand that logic.

The second value-based assumption is that the objective of functional assessment is not just to define and eliminate undesirable behaviors but to understand the structure and function of those behaviors in order to teach and promote effective alternatives. The goal of behavioral support is to create environments and patterns of support around people that make their problem behaviors irrelevant, ineffective, or inefficient. We hope the information you obtain by using the materials and procedures presented in this handbook will make you more effective at identifying (a) unnecessary situations that prompt undesirable behaviors you can eliminate or modify; (b) new or alternative skills you can teach that will be more effective and efficient than the undesirable behaviors, thereby making them unnecessary; and (c) effective staff responses to the undesirable behaviors.

The third value-based assumption is that functional assessment is a process for looking at relationships between behavior and the environment. It is *not* simply a "review" of the person with problem behaviors. Problem behaviors cannot be addressed without looking at the broader environmental contexts within which they occur. A functional assessment should produce information about (a) the undesirable behaviors, (b) relevant structural features of the environment, and (c) the behavior of support providers and patterns of support such as staffing patterns. A functional assessment is as much an analysis of the environment (schedules, activity patterns, curriculum, support staff, physical settings) as it is of the behavior of the person. Do not allow a functional assessment to become a process that "blames" the person for behaving in undesirable ways.

CHAPTER TWO

Functional Assessment and Analysis Strategies

This handbook presents three strategies for collecting functional assessment and analysis information: interviews with relevant persons, systematic direct observation of behavior, and systematic manipulations of environmental contingencies—that is, functional analysis. We have used these strategies in different ways. Often we start with an interview, move to systematic direct observation, and complete the analysis with systematic manipulations. In many situations, however, interviews and systematic observations have been the primary means for achieving the desired outcomes of describing the undesirable behavior and identifying predictors and maintaining consequences. This section of the handbook presents the procedures for each of these options.

The Functional Assessment Interview (FAI)

Behavior can be very complex. Researchers, direct support personnel, and families can identify many things in a person's learning history and physical makeup that can affect his or her behavior. A major purpose of functional assessment interviews is to collect information about events that influence problem behavior. Your task is to narrow the focus to those events that may be very important for the individual receiving support. The interview is not a functional analysis in the technical sense (that is, it does not empirically document functional relationships). The interview does, however, help to identify those variables—settings, events, activities—that can be targeted through direct observation and/or systematic manipulation strategies.

Who Should Be Interviewed?

Two groups can participate in interviews. One group consists of teachers, support staff, parents and family members, and other relevant persons who work with or know the individual well. The other group is the individuals who are exhibiting behaviors of concern. Several factors will determine the interview participation of the second group, such as their interest, availability, willingness, and ability to engage in more complex conversational interactions. To gain information about some individuals, talking primarily with teachers, parents, and support staff will make the most sense. However, when it seems appropriate and productive, you should include the individual of concern in the process to the greatest extent possible (see the section later in this chapter titled "Including the Individual: The Student-Directed Functional Assessment Interview" for an example of how this can be done). When interviewing teachers, parents, and other informants, you should talk with at least one and preferably two or more people who have daily contact with the individual. The individual of concern also may participate in these interviews or can be interviewed separately.

Teachers and direct service personnel have used the interview process and Functional Assessment Interview form also as a self-interview. (An example and description of the form appears later in the chapter.) For example, a teacher and his or her classroom assistants can set aside time to discuss and answer the interview questions as part of a self-guided process.

What Are the Outcomes of a Functional Assessment Interview?

The four main outcomes of a functional assessment interview are similar to the outcomes for the functional assessment process as a whole (see Box 1.1):

1. Description of the behaviors of concern
2. Identification of general and more immediate physical and environmental factors that predict the occurrence and nonoccurrence of the problem behaviors
3. Identification of the potential functions of the behaviors in relation to the outcomes or consequences that are maintaining them
4. Development of summary statements describing relationships among situations, behaviors, and their functions

In addition, the interview can be an opportunity to collect information about a range of other things that will be helpful in developing support programs for an individual, such as the person's communicative abilities and items and activities that are effective reinforcers.

How Long Does the Interview Take?

A functional assessment interview with two staff members concerning a complex behavior pattern may take 45 to 90 minutes. Our experience has shown that the time required to complete the process can vary considerably from one interview to another. Use of the Functional Assessment Interview (FAI) form should help to keep the interview focused and efficient. Some cases, however, may require more lengthy discussion.

Using the Functional Assessment Interview (FAI) Form

The FAI is divided into 11 major sections. You may wish to take a moment to examine the blank form presented in Appendix B. We describe each section of the form below.

A. Describe the behaviors Section A provides an opportunity to describe the undesirable behaviors clearly. The two questions in this section are designed to accomplish three objectives. The first is to encourage the interviewee to list not only the most undesirable behavior but also *all* behaviors that are a problem. Behavior support plans often will be designed around classes of behavior (such as all those behaviors maintained by the same consequence). For example, if a student's screaming, vomiting, throwing things, and running away are all maintained by teacher attention, the behavior support plan will address *all* these behaviors together. To facilitate this process, the interviewer needs to gather information about all the problem behaviors an individual performs. Problem behaviors can be extremely dangerous (severe self-biting), mildly undesirable (pushing materials away), or functionally irrelevant (repetitive movements that do not interfere with ongoing activities). We have found, however, that a person with severe problem behavior seldom performs only one or two behaviors that cause concern. Possibly only one or two behaviors are dangerous and receive major attention, but it is important for you to obtain a list of the full range of behaviors that you perceive as obstacles and that the person performs regularly.

The second objective of Section A is to facilitate the operational description of the behaviors. Question A.1 provides room for listing (a) a label or "title" for a behavior, (b) a brief description of the topography or physical movements that are performed, (c) the basic frequency with which the behavior is performed, (d) the length of time the behavior continues and (e) a description of the intensity of the behavior, which allows the interviewer to record his or her perceptions of the level of danger or serious effects presented by the behavior. The key is to provide a short descriptive picture of each behavior listed.

The third objective of Section A is to identify the extent to which the different behaviors occur together or in a predictable sequence or chain. We have found this information to be of tremendous value in building behavioral support plans. Behaviors that occur together often are members of the same class—that is, they serve the same behavioral function. In question A.2, you are eliciting information that will show that different behaviors may be in a similar class. This will indicate that these behaviors should be treated similarly in a behavior support plan.

B. Define potential ecological/setting events

Ecological or setting events are those aspects of a person's environment or daily routines that do not necessarily happen immediately before or after the undesirable behaviors but still affect whether these behaviors are performed; that is, events may occur in the morning but still influence problem behaviors in the afternoon. In more precise behavioral terminology, these events are *establishing operations*. The seven items below provide an overview of setting events we have found to be important for understanding the behavior of specific individuals.

1. *Medications:* Determine whether a person is taking a prescription medication. Note the number of times per day the medication is given and the dosage given each time. Try to learn how these medications might affect his or her alertness, confusion, responsiveness, and so on.

2. *Medical or physical problems:* Does the person have allergies, asthma, rashes, infections, or other conditions that may cause pain or discomfort?

3. *Sleep cycles:* Determine how long the person typically sleeps in a 24-hour period, when he or she sleeps, and the duration of sleep periods if there is more than one per day.

4. *Eating routines and diet:* Determine how often the person eats, the approximate number of calories consumed per day, preferences or dislikes for specific foods, and any dietary restrictions that are important. Sometimes, simply allowing the person to eat smaller, more frequent meals may have a dramatic impact on problem behavior.

5. *Daily schedule:* Obtain an outline of the person's basic daily schedule of activities (5.a). The two follow-up questions (5.b and 5.c) are aimed at collecting information about how *predictable* the activities are and how often the person has a chance to *make choices* about activities. These are aspects of people's lives that have been shown to influence the occurrence of problem behaviors.

6. *Numbers of people:* Determine the number of other people in the work, school, and home environments and whether this number seems relevant to the person's behavior. Greater numbers of people, particularly in smaller spaces, usually increase the levels of noise, crowding, and general confusion. Many people, both with and without disabilities, may have difficulty functioning well in such situations.

7. *Staffing patterns and interactions:* Many persons with disabilities receive substantial support in their home, school, work, or other community settings. The ways in which staff provide such support are critical in the success of the support plan. When you ask questions in this area, you are trying to learn the typical staff pattern or ratio the person experiences and whether types of staff behavior and interactions appear to affect the behaviors of concern.

C. Define the immediate antecedent events (predictors) for occurrences and nonoccurrences of the problem behavior Ask questions about specific situations in which the problem behaviors happen, including *when* and *where* they occur, *whom* the person is with, and *what specific activities* are problematic. Difficult behaviors are often related to such aspects of a setting. Learning about these relationships can help you predict the pattern of a person's problem behaviors—what may be "setting them up."

1. *Time of day:* Do the behaviors consistently occur or *not* occur during specific periods during the day? Such information is useful in focusing on and analyzing the particular circumstances during problematic and nonproblematic periods.
2. *Physical setting:* Do the behaviors occur more or less often in particular physical settings (a certain area of a classroom, a specific work site, a playground, a bathroom)? What characteristics of those settings may affect the behaviors?
3. *People:* Do problem behaviors occur or *not* occur more consistently in the presence of particular people? Along with time and place, the presence or absence of certain people—family members, staff persons—may predict whether the behaviors will occur.
4. *Activity:* Are specific activities related to the behaviors? This information can suggest the types of demands and activity outcomes that the person may not like.

One or more of these aspects may be more powerful than the others; that is, the behaviors may occur whenever a certain activity is presented, no matter who does it or where it occurs. However, although you ask about time, place, persons, and activities separately, keep in mind that combinations of these may often be important. The problem behaviors may occur during a certain period when a particular person is around and engaging in a particular activity in a certain place.

The remaining three questions in Section C (Questions 5, 6, and 7) ask about idiosyncratic or very specific situations or events that may be important to the person involved. These might include particular requests made to the individual, taking him or her from one activity/setting to another, requiring him or her to wait for access to a desired object/activity, asking the individual to stop doing something particularly enjoyable, and so on. Your informants can probably identify one very important thing they feel would be most reliable in making the problem behaviors occur (Question 6). When answering these questions, remember that identifying situations in which the problem behaviors are *unlikely* will be as valuable as identifying those in which the behaviors are highly predictable.

This section of the interview should help people understand that difficult behaviors are very often situation-specific; they occur in some situations and not in others. Understanding the situations in which behaviors occur helps both in building a support plan and in avoiding the trap of thinking of a person as "having" a difficult behavior.

D. Identify the consequences or outcomes of the undesirable behaviors that may be maintaining them The earlier sections of the interview focused on obtaining information about features of a person's environment that predict the occurrence and nonoccurrence of problem behaviors. Another important aspect of behavior-environment relationships concerns the types of results that behaviors produce for a person—the *functions* they appear to serve. We assume that any behavior that occurs repeatedly is serving some useful function or producing some type of reinforcement.

One way to think of this is that behaviors may serve two major types of functions: to *obtain* something desirable and to *avoid* or *escape* something undesirable. In more technical terms, behaviors maintained by obtaining desirable things are examples of *positive reinforcement;* behaviors maintained by escaping or avoiding undesirable things are examples of *negative reinforcement.* Figure 2.1 expands this framework for organizing the

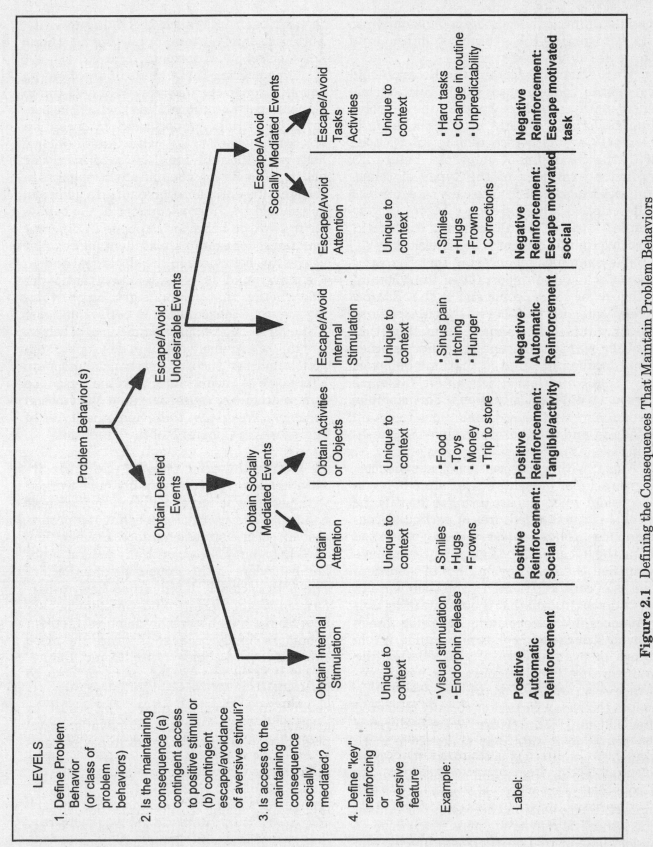

Figure 2.1 Defining the Consequences That Maintain Problem Behaviors

possible functions of problem behaviors into six categories—three under "Obtain" and three under "Escape/Avoid."

Under both the Obtain and Escape/Avoid categories, consequences can be further classified with regard to whether they involve *internal/private* events or *external/socially mediated* events, which require interactions with the environment or people. Figure 2.1 provides examples of the types of consequences that might fit into each category and a descriptive label for each category (for example, Positive Reinforcement: Automatic, Positive Reinforcement: Tangible/activity).

The examples given show that the *same outcomes* may be important in the "Obtain" category for some people and in the "Escape/Avoid" category for others—that is, what one person wants to obtain may be something that another wants to escape or avoid. Another issue to keep in mind is that one behavior may serve *multiple functions* for the same person in different situations. For example, screaming may be used sometimes to obtain attention and at other times to avoid a difficult task.

Along with categories of consequences, Figure 2.1 also presents a set of steps or levels to consider when you are trying to identify the *specific* important features of particular consequences. These questions are presented along the left side of the figure. Once you have identified the behavior or class of behaviors that is of concern (Level 1), you then want to try to detect (a) whether the maintaining consequences involve obtaining desirable things or events, or escaping or avoiding undesirable things or events (Level 2); (b) whether the maintaining consequences are more concerned with internal or private events than events that are external or socially mediated (Level 3); and (c) the critical or *key* features of the things or events that make them more desirable or undesirable (Level 4). For example, for some persons social attention may be desirable if it involves some type of physical contact (hugs, pats on the back). For others, task or activity demands may be aversive or undesirable primarily when they involve fine motor movements, such as having to write, buttoning shirt buttons, or putting together a small object on an assembly line.

Remembering these kinds of questions as you go through the interview will help you to target important information that will be useful in planning support and intervention strategies. Question D.1 of the interview form asks what the individual of concern may be getting or avoiding when he or she engages in the identified problem behaviors. In addition, you should tie the consequence of the behavior to how the behavior happens in *different situations*. For example, a student may exhibit aggressive behaviors in the classroom and on the playground. It would be important to decide whether that person is getting or avoiding the same consequence in both situations.

Being specific about the functions of behaviors can be extremely useful in developing support strategies, such as teaching appropriate alternative behaviors that can get the person the same outcomes or consequences as the problem behaviors. We discuss these and other types of approaches in Chapter 3 of the handbook.

E. Define the efficiency of the undesirable behaviors You probably have worked with people who have exhibited inconsistent behavior. They sometimes behave appropriately in certain situations, such as when they need help, but also occasionally exhibit problem behaviors in the same type of situation. The person clearly has learned how to perform *both* appropriate and problem behaviors. Sometimes he or she displays problem behaviors simply because they are the more *efficient* way to achieve an outcome. Behaviors that are more *efficient* are more likely to be performed. These are behaviors that (a) require less physical effort, (b) result in quicker and more consistent payoffs, or (c) produce results quickly. For example, screaming or head-hitting might require less effort for a particular person than engaging in appropriate communicative behaviors (speaking, signing, using a communication board). Screaming or head-hitting also may draw attention more rapidly. The questions in this section help you focus on the kind of information you need to obtain about the identified problem behaviors.

F. What functional alternative behaviors does the person already know how to do? An important and very useful strategy involves teaching and/or reinforcing persons for engaging in appropriate alternative behaviors. The question in Section F of the FAI form solicits specific information about whether the individual already knows behaviors he or she can perform that could produce the same outcomes or consequences as the problem behaviors. For example, a person may have shown the ability to sometimes ask for help or ask for a break from an activity in an appropriate manner by talking or signing. Knowing this will help you decide whether instruction needs to focus on teaching new skills or on trying to prompt and reinforce the skills the person already has.

G. What are the primary ways the person communicates with other people? In thinking about appropriate alternative behaviors, communication is the single most important skill to consider for people with severe problem behaviors. If support is to be effective, you must understand the ways in which a person communicates important information to others in the environment. Section G of the interview first allows you to record basic information on the person's typical communication strategies. It then provides a chart for summarizing answers to questions about the different types of responses used by persons to achieve several common communicative functions. Questions G.3.a to G.3.d solicit information about the individual's receptive abilities.

H. What are things you should do and things you should avoid in working with and supporting this person? Section H of the interview probes for general information about the kinds of approaches that *do* and *do not* work well with the person during activities or teaching sessions. For example, some

people might prefer a faster pace, louder and livelier interactions, constant encouragement, and so on; others might prefer a slower pace and a quieter, less bubbly person with whom to interact.

I. What are things that the person likes and are reinforcing for him or her? It is very important to identify effective reinforcers (objects, events, activities) if you are to develop successful support strategies. In asking questions about preferred things, you should learn which events or activities the person seeks spontaneously and which things others typically provide. Staff reports can be good indicators of functional reinforcers but the things a person seeks voluntarily may be an even better indicator. Although interviews can produce useful information, a comprehensive support plan will often require that you directly test a person's preferences with regard to reinforcing objects, activities, and events. Such assessments typically involve exposing individuals to a variety of potential reinforcers, including edibles, toys/objects, entertainment (music, TV, movies), games, outings, domestic activities, or grooming. Through such exposure, you might decide which categories and specific items the person prefers most by observing the amount of time he or she spends with them, or by examining other indicators of interest. (See Appendix A for relevant references on methods of reinforcer assessment.)

Identifying the current functions of problem behaviors may also be useful in determining and selecting reinforcers. For example, if a person consistently exhibits difficult behaviors to escape from situations, free time with no demands would presumably be a reinforcing consequence. If a person consistently engages in such behaviors to obtain particular objects or social interaction/attention, then such objects or interactions should be powerful reinforcers that could be used in a support program.

J. What do you know about the history of the undesirable behaviors, the pro-

grams that have been attempted to decrease or eliminate them, and the effects of those programs? Learning about the types of interventions others have attempted and the effects these have had can provide clues about the things that influence the behaviors. For example, if you learn that a time-out program was tried and *increased* the frequency of a behavior, this result might suggest that the behavior is motivated by escaping or avoiding situations or demands. Often it may be hard to obtain clear and reliable information about what has been tried and how well it worked or did not work. Nevertheless, trying is important.

K. Develop summary statements for each major predictor and/or consequence Section K provides a place for you to pull together and summarize the interview information into one or more specific statements. You should develop an individual summary statement for each major category of predictor events or consequences that are identified in the interview. The next section of the book provides more detail about and examples of such statements. These summary statements will be important in guiding later systematic direct observations and in developing support plans.

Developing Summary Statements

The fourth main outcome of the interview process requires integrating the interview information into "summary statements" about the problem behaviors. These summary statements will be important with regard to both moving into other assessment activities and eventually developing behavior support plans.

Summary statements describe three components: (a) a situation—setting events and immediate antecedents—in which problem behaviors occur; (b) the behaviors that are occurring; and (c) the function the behaviors serve, or the reinforcing outcomes they produce, in that situation. Summary statements integrate the information you have gathered with regard to behaviors, antecedents, and consequences that are maintaining the behaviors. You should attempt to develop summary statements for (a) each behavior or class of behaviors that appears to serve a particular function and (b) each type of particular situation in which that behavior or class of behaviors occurs. For example, you might end up with two summary statements regarding a person's self-injurious head-hitting and hand biting. One statement would deal with the behaviors and their occurrence during small group instructional activities; the other statement would deal with their occurrence during the bus ride to and from school. Taking this approach will be important to ensure that you are dealing with the different behavioral functions that may be served in different situations. Box 2.1 presents some examples of summary statements; note that each statement has the components described above (situation, behaviors, and functions/outcomes). Examples 1, 2, and 6 include situations with both immediate and distant events affecting problem behavior. The summary statement elements are labeled in Example 1; conduct a self-test by labeling the summary statement elements for Examples 2–6.

Figure 2.2 presents a Functional Assessment Interview form completed while the interviewer was talking with teachers working with an elementary school student named Curtis. Curtis is 11 years old and carries the diagnoses of moderate to severe intellectual disabilities and hyperactivity disorder. Curtis has a history of seizures. He is in a regular fourth-grade class with 27 other students. His regular education teacher receives support from a consultant and from a part-time teaching assistant. Read the interview carefully, keeping in mind the four desired outcomes: (a) defining the behaviors; (b) defining potentially relevant features that predict the occurrence and nonoccurrence of the behaviors; (c) defining the potential functions served by the behaviors (maintaining consequences); and (d) developing summary statements.

BOX 2.1 Examples of Summary Statements Based on Interview Information

1. _____ *Immediate situation* _____
   "When Perry is getting little attention in a large group in the classroom,
   _____ *Problem behavior* _____ ____ *Maintaining function* ____
   he is likely to shout profanities and throw things to get peer attention.
   _____ *Distant event (setting event)* _____
   The less attention Perry has received during the day, the more likely this pattern is _____
   to occur."
2. "When Monique is asked to do independent assembly jobs at her work station, she is likely to tear up materials and hit her supervisor to escape from the task demands. This pattern is more likely if she slept fewer than 4 hours the night before."
3. "When Jacqueline is prompted to stop playing with the computer or record player in the play area, she is likely to fall on the floor and scream to try to continue to be allowed to play with the items."
4. "In situations with low levels of activity or attention at home, José will rock and begin to chew his wrist to produce self-stimulation."
5. "When José is asked to dress himself or do other nonpreferred self-care routines, he will begin to chew on his wrist to try to escape from the task demands."
6. "When Andrea begins to have difficulty with a reading or math assignment, she will put her head down, refuse to respond, and close her books to try to avoid having to complete the assignment. The likelihood of this pattern increases if Andrea has received teacher reprimands earlier in the day."

Including the Individual: The Student-Directed Functional Assessment Interview

To date, functional assessment procedures have been most often used to design support for persons with moderate to severe intellectual disabilities. Recently, however, Lee Kern, Glen Dunlap, and others have demonstrated successful interventions based on functional assessments with children who have emotional and behavioral disorders, conduct disorders, mild intellectual disabilities, and brain injury as well as with developmentally typical children.

The success of linking functional assessment and intervention for more intellectually able individuals raises the possibility of collecting information *from the person performing the problem behavior*. We believe that important information regarding the development of support plans can be obtained this way. Our clinical experience and that of others suggest that many students can clearly (a) state preferences for activities or items, (b) describe complaints about assigned work, (c) request alternative activities, (d) point out personal distractions, and (e) describe difficulties with peers. To the extent that these statements are accurate and consistent, personally provided information can supplement information obtained from teachers, parents, or others.

As one approach to including individuals directly in the functional assessment process, we have developed a Student-Directed Functional Assessment Interview. The title of the interview emphasizes that our development and field-test efforts to date have been done in elementary and middle schools.

Who Should Be Interviewed?

Any student who can provide reliable information can contribute functional assessment

FUNCTIONAL ASSESSMENT INTERVIEW (FAI)

Person of concern *Curtis Jackson* _____ Age *11* _____ Sex Ⓜ F

Date of interview *5/7/96* _____ Interviewer *Jane Wolf* _____

Respondents *Alex McDonnell, Sharon Kiefer, John Mayhew* _____

A. DESCRIBE THE BEHAVIORS.

1. For each of the behaviors of concern, define the topography (how it is performed), frequency (how often it occurs per day, week, or month), duration (how long it lasts when it occurs), and intensity (how damaging or destructive the behaviors are when they occur).

	Behavior	Topography	Frequency	Duration	Intensity
a.	Yelling	Uses obscenities	5–6 times/week	5–10 seconds	Loud
b.	Throwing objects	Books/materials against the wall	5–6 times/week	15–30 seconds	Will dent wall
c.	Pinching/ scratching peers	Grabs hand/arm and twists/digs	4–5 times/week	5–10 seconds	Bruises and bleeding
d.	Pounding/ slapping desk	Hits with open or closed hand	2–3 times/day	5–10 seconds	Easily audible
e.	Calling out	Repeatedly says teacher's name	5–6 times/day	5–10 seconds	Easily audible
f.	Scratching own arm	Repeatedly drags nails up and down	8–10 times/day	5–10 seconds	Can lead to bleeding
g.					
h.					
i.					
j.					

2. Which of the behaviors described above are likely to occur together in some way? Do they occur about the same time? In some kind of predictable sequence or "chain"? In response to the same type of situation?

   Yelling and throwing objects; Pounding/slapping and calling out _____

   _____

1

Figure 2.2 Completed Functional Assessment Interview Form for Curtis Jackson

B. DEFINE ECOLOGICAL EVENTS (SETTING EVENTS) THAT PREDICT OR SET UP THE PROBLEM BEHAVIORS.

1. What *medications* is the person taking (if any), and how do you believe these may affect his or her behavior?

   Tegretol to control seizures (500 mg. twice daily); may be causing increased thirst and

   requests for water/drinks, and arm rash/itching (taking Benadryl, 50 mg/day; causing

   sleepiness?)

2. What *medical* or *physical conditions (if any)* does the person experience that may affect his or her behavior (e.g., asthma, allergies, rashes, sinus infections, seizures, problems related to menstruation)?

   Some kind of skin problem on arm (itching, occasional rash); seems to be causing arm

   scratching; related to Tegretol?

3. Describe the *sleep patterns* of the individual and the extent to which these patterns may affect his or her behavior.

   Generally sleeps well (7–8 hrs. per night); occasional sleepiness during day due to Benadryl?

4. Describe the *eating routines and diet* of the person and the extent to which these may affect his or her behavior.

   No consistent problems; need to monitor/limit intake of sweets (e.g., soda, candy, cookies).

   Occasionally will refuse breakfast, which can lead to more problems in morning

5a. Briefly list below the person's typical daily schedule of activities. (Check the boxes by those activities the person enjoys and those activities most associated with problems.)

Enjoys	Problems			Enjoys	Problems	
☒	☐	6:00	*Up at 6:30, shower & dress*	☒	☐	2:00 *Community skills training*
☒	☐	7:00	*Breakfast; catch bus at 7:45*	☒	☐	3:00 *Catch bus for home*
☐	☐	8:00	*Arrv school 8:15; class 8:30*	☒	☐	4:00 *Snack, leisure time*
☐	☒	9:00	*Reading/Language arts*	☒	☐	5:00 *Home chores, dinner prep*
☐	☒	10:00	*Math skills group*	☒	☐	6:00 *Dinner with family*
☒	☐	11:00	*School jobs (cpy rm/rcyclg)*	☒	☐	7:00 *Rm cleanup, leisure time*
☐	☒	12:00	*Lunch/cafeteria/rcss to 1:00*	☒	☐	8:00 *Rm cleanup, leisure time*
☐	☒	1:00	*P.E./hygiene skills*	☒	☐	9:00 *Bedtime routine; bed 9:30*

2

Figure 2.2 *(continued)*

5b. To what extent are the activities on the daily schedule *predictable* for the person, with regard to what will be happening, when it will occur, with whom, and for how long?

Class schedule on board; verbal reminders

5c. To what extent does the person have the opportunity during the day to *make choices* about his or her activities and reinforcing events? (e.g., food, clothing, social companions, leisure activities)

Not much; can choose school job each day

6. How many other persons are typically around the individual at home, school, or work (including staff, classmates, and housemates)? Does the person typically seem bothered in situations that are more *crowded and noisy?*

Classroom has 11 other students; doesn't seem bothered by noise/crowds, but needs more

attention when it's busy

7. What is the pattern of *staffing support* that the person receives in home, school, work, and other settings (e.g., 1:1, 2:1)? Do you believe that the *number* of staff, the *training* of staff, or their *social interactions with the person* affect the problem behaviors?

Child/teacher ratio about 4:1; Curtis does better when he gets more individualized attention;

likes all 3 staff

C. DEFINE SPECIFIC IMMEDIATE ANTECEDENT EVENTS THAT PREDICT WHEN THE BEHAVIORS ARE *LIKELY* AND *NOT* LIKELY TO OCCUR.

1. *Times of Day: When* are the behaviors most and least likely to happen?

Most likely: *Most behaviors more likely in the morning and at lunch, recess, and P.E.*

Least likely: *Least likely in afternoon after P.E.*

3

Figure 2.2 *(continued)*

2. *Settings: Where* are the behaviors most and least likely to happen?

Most likely: *Most likely in classroom; pinching/scratching peers more likely on playground and during P.E. in gym*

Least likely: *In the community*

3. *People: With whom* are the behaviors most and least likely to happen?

Most likely: *About equal across staff; seems more related to activities*

Least likely: _____

4. *Activity: What activities* are most and least likely to produce the behaviors?

Most likely: *Reading (e.g., sightwords); Math (e.g., counting objects); groups with little 1:1 attention; games (recess and P.E.)*

Least likely: *School jobs; community outings*

5. Are there particular or idiosyncratic situations or events not listed above that sometimes seem to "set off" the behaviors, such as particular demands, noises, lights, clothing?

Gets upset when asked/reminded not to scratch arms; often responds with obscenities

6. What *one thing* could you do that would most likely make the undesirable behaviors occur?

Ask Curtis to sound out long list of sightwords

7. Briefly describe how the person's behavior would be affected if . . .
   a. You asked him or her to perform a difficult task.

   More likely to yell, throw stuff

   b. You interrupted a desired activity, such as eating ice cream or watching TV.

   More likely to refuse, yell

   c. You unexpectedly changed his or her typical routine or schedule of activities.

   Not usually a problem

4

Figure 2.2 *(continued)*

d. She or he wanted something but wasn't able to get it (e.g., a food item up on a shelf).

May repeatedly ask for item

e. You didn't pay attention to the person or left her or him alone for a while (e.g., 15 minutes).

More likely to call out, pound / slap desk

D. IDENTIFY THE CONSEQUENCES OR OUTCOMES OF THE PROBLEM BEHAVIORS THAT MAY BE MAINTAINING THEM (I.E., THE FUNCTIONS THEY SERVE FOR THE PERSON IN PARTICULAR SITUATIONS).

1. Think of each of the behaviors listed in Section A, and try to identify the *specific* consequences or outcomes the person gets when the behaviors occur in different situations.

	Behavior	Particular situations	What exactly does he or she get?	What exactly does she or he avoid?
a.	*Yelling*	*Nonpreferred tasks / interruptions*		*Doing task / interruption*
b.	*Throwing objects*	*Nonpreferred tasks / interruptions*		*Doing task / interruption*
c.	*Pinching / scratching peers*	*Wants item / object (e.g., ball)*	*Gets item*	
d.	*Pounding / slapping*	*Group work (little attention)*	*Attention (peers and teachers)*	
e.	*Calling out*	*Group work (little attention)*	*Attention (peers and teachers)*	
f.	*Scratching arm*	*Across many / all situations*		*Relief from itching?*
g.				
h.				
i.				
j.				

E. CONSIDER THE OVERALL *EFFICIENCY* OF THE PROBLEM BEHAVIORS. EFFICIENCY IS THE COMBINED RESULT OF (A) HOW MUCH *PHYSICAL EFFORT* IS REQUIRED, (B) *HOW OFTEN* THE BEHAVIOR IS PERFORMED BEFORE IT IS REWARDED, AND (C) *HOW LONG* THE PERSON MUST WAIT TO GET THE REWARD.

	Low Efficiency				High Efficiency
Yelling / throwing	1	2	③	4	5
Pinching / scratching	1	②	3	4	5
Pounding / slapping / calling out	1	2	3	4	⑤
Scratching arm	1	2	3	4	⑤
	1	2	3	4	5

5

Figure 2.2 *(continued)*

F. WHAT *FUNCTIONAL ALTERNATIVE* BEHAVIORS DOES THE PERSON ALREADY KNOW HOW TO DO?

   1. What socially appropriate behaviors or skills can the person already perform that may generate the same outcomes or reinforcers produced by the problem behaviors?

   Can raise hand; can say phrases like "Don't like" and "Want"

   _____

   _____

G. WHAT ARE THE PRIMARY WAYS THE PERSON COMMUNICATES WITH OTHER PEOPLE?

   1. What are the general expressive communication strategies used by or available to the person? These might include vocal speech, signs/gestures, communication boards/books, or electronic devices. How consistently are the strategies used?

   Curtis uses 1- or 2-word spoken phrases for many things, sometimes in combination with gestures (will try to point at things he wants); however, his speech is often fairly difficult to understand.

   2. On the following chart, indicate the behaviors the person uses to achieve the communicative outcomes listed:

Communicative Functions	Complex speech (sentences)	Multiple-word phrases	One-word utterances	Echolalia	Other vocalizing	Complex signing	Single signs	Pointing	Leading	Shakes head	Grabs/reaches	Gives objects	Increased movement	Moves close to you	Moves away or leaves	Fixed gaze	Facial expression	Aggression	Self-injury	Other
Request attention			x		x															x
Request help																x	x			
Request preferred food/objects/activities			x					x			x							x		
Request break			x												x					x
Show you something or some place			x					x	x											
Indicate physical pain (headache, illness)																				?
Indicate confusion or unhappiness					x												x			?
Protest or reject a situation or activity		x			x															x

6

Figure 2.2 *(continued)*

3. With regard to the person's receptive communication, or ability to understand other persons . . .
   a. Does the person follow spoken requests or instructions? If so, approximately how many? (List if only a few.)

   Large number of one-step requests; smaller number of two-step

   b. Does the person respond to signed or gestural requests or instructions? If so, approximately how many? (List if only a few.)

   Can follow pointing gestures/prompts

   c. Is the person able to imitate if you provide physical models for various tasks or activities? (List if only a few.)

   Imitates physical modeling of many things

   d. How does the person typically indicate *yes or no* when asked if she or he wants something, wants to go somewhere, and so on?

   Will say yes or no; but not always clear if it's accurate

H. WHAT ARE THINGS YOU *SHOULD DO* AND THINGS YOU *SHOULD AVOID* IN WORKING WITH AND SUPPORTING THIS PERSON?
   1. What things can you do to improve the likelihood that a teaching session or other activity will go well with this person?

   Slower pace; lots of encouragement; joking/playful attitude; positive voice tone

   2. What things should you avoid that might interfere with or disrupt a teaching session or activity with this person?

   Faster pace; reprimanding tone of voice; rapid repeated requests and/or prompts

I. WHAT ARE THINGS THE PERSON LIKES AND ARE REINFORCING FOR HIM OR HER?
   1. *Food items:* *Sweets (candy, cookies, ice cream, soda); chips/nuts; applesauce; hot dogs; crackers*

7

Figure 2.2 *(continued)*

2. *Toys and objects:* <u>Space action figures and dolls; Gameboy-type toys; felt-tip pens/</u>

<u>markers; pogs and marbles; computer games</u>

_____

3. *Activities at home:* <u>Help parents with outdoor chores; push skateboard and wagon around</u>

<u>with sibling; play catch with father; TV</u>

_____

4. *Activities/outings in the community:* <u>Fast-food restaurants; miniature golf; go-carts; duck</u>

<u>pond; snow sledding/tubing; swim at the YMCA</u>

_____

5. *Other:* <u>Movies (will tolerate for short periods); bus rides</u>

_____

_____

J. WHAT DO YOU KNOW ABOUT THE HISTORY OF THE UNDESIRABLE BEHAVIORS, THE PROGRAMS THAT HAVE BEEN ATTEMPTED TO DECREASE OR ELIMINATE THEM, AND THE EFFECTS OF THOSE PROGRAMS?

Behavior	How long has this been a problem?	Programs	Effects
1. <u>Yelling curses</u>	*1–2 years*	*Ignoring or reprimands*	*Not much*
2. <u>Throwing objects</u>	*1–2 years*	*Reprimands and time-out*	*Some decrease*
3. <u>Pinching/scratching</u>	*6 months*	*Apologize and time-out*	*Not much*
4. <u>Pounding/slapping</u>	*1 year*	*Ignoring or time-out*	*Some decrease*
5. <u>Calling out</u>	*1 year*	*Ignoring or reprimands; told to wait*	*Some decrease*
6. <u>Arm scratching</u>	*6 months*	*Prompts to stop; Benadryl*	*Not much*
7. _____			
8. _____			
9. _____			
10. _____			

8

Figure 2.2 *(continued)*

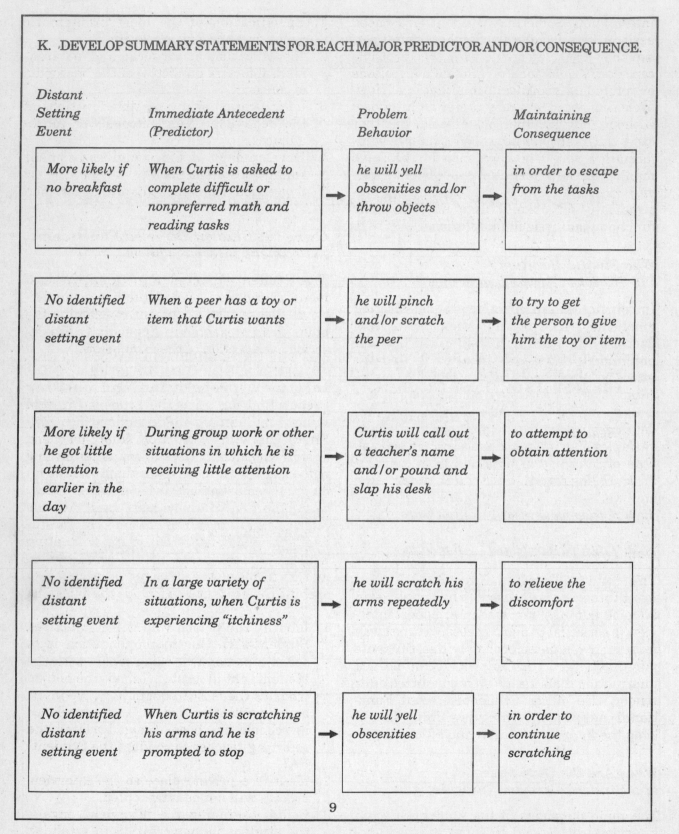

K. DEVELOP SUMMARY STATEMENTS FOR EACH MAJOR PREDICTOR AND/OR CONSEQUENCE.

Distant Setting Event	Immediate Antecedent (Predictor)	Problem Behavior	Maintaining Consequence
More likely if no breakfast	*When Curtis is asked to complete difficult or nonpreferred math and reading tasks*	*he will yell obscenities and/or throw objects*	*in order to escape from the tasks*
No identified distant setting event	*When a peer has a toy or item that Curtis wants*	*he will pinch and/or scratch the peer*	*to try to get the person to give him the toy or item*
More likely if he got little attention earlier in the day	*During group work or other situations in which he is receiving little attention*	*Curtis will call out a teacher's name and/or pound and slap his desk*	*to attempt to obtain attention*
No identified distant setting event	*In a large variety of situations, when Curtis is experiencing "itchiness"*	*he will scratch his arms repeatedly*	*to relieve the discomfort*
No identified distant setting event	*When Curtis is scratching his arms and he is prompted to stop*	*he will yell obscenities*	*in order to continue scratching*

9

Figure 2.2 *(continued)*

information. Sometimes students may need assistance from a family member or staff person they are comfortable with. These people can clarify questions or provide suggestions or reminders about certain situations. However, some students may prefer an interview without additional persons present. In either case, the quality or accuracy of interview information would be confirmed in the same manner as the Functional Assessment Interview described above—that is, through systematic observational data or systematic functional analysis manipulations.

Who Should Conduct the Student-Directed Interview?

In some cases, an effective student-directed functional assessment interview can be conducted by the student's parent or teacher. Our preliminary experience, however, is that the interview occurs more quickly and elicits more substantive information from the student if it is conducted by a person with whom the student does *not* have a negative history. Many variables may influence the accuracy and volume of information obtained from student-directed functional assessment interviews, and we believe selection of the interviewer may be one of the more important factors.

How Long Does the Interview Take?

The Student-Directed Functional Assessment Interview is designed to be completed in 20 to 40 minutes. For students, a short interview is essential to avoid excessive time away from their regular school activities. Students may have more time to provide the needed information if the interview is conducted after school. Use of the Student-Directed Functional Assessment Interview form should keep the interview focused and efficient.

What Are the Outcomes of a Student-Directed Interview?

The main outcomes of the student-directed interview correspond to those of the Functional Assessment Interview (FAI):

1. Specification of the most problematic times or situations across the day
2. Identification of physical and environmental factors predictive of the behaviors of concern
3. Identification of the possible functions of the behaviors (their outcomes or consequences)
4. Development of functional assessment summary statements
5. Suggestions for components of a support plan

Using the Student-Directed Functional Assessment Interview Form

The Student-Directed Functional Assessment Interview is divided into five major sections. Please take a moment to examine the blank form presented in Appendix C. We describe each section of the form below.

Interview preparation and opening
Preparation for using the Student-Directed Functional Assessment Interview (Student-FAI) begins with referral from family, teachers, or staff who identify the student as performing patterns of problem behavior that warrant individualized behavioral intervention. In most cases, the FAI will have been used with the referring adult to identify patterns of the student's problem behavior before a meeting with the student is scheduled. With this information in place, the steps for preparing and opening the Student-FAI include the following:

1. Identify the person who will conduct the Student-FAI. Our recommendation is to select a person who has rapport with the student, but in most cases, not the person who has the most frequent negative interactions with the student. Our experience in schools has been to avoid asking the referring teacher to conduct the Student-FAI.
2. Identify a private place so the interview process will not be interrupted.
3. Before beginning the interview, engage the student in conversation to establish comfort and rapport.

4. Inform the student of the purpose of the interview and stress the need for candid answers. As you go on, if you feel strongly that the student might be giving false information or is reluctant to speak, you may wish to end the interview calmly and ask to finish it at another time. You may also provide gentle reminders to the student about information you have obtained from adults in the setting.

Define the behaviors of concern Section II provides an opportunity to define the behaviors that are problematic. The student should be encouraged to list not only the most problematic behavior but also *all* behaviors he or she *thinks* are problematic ("those behaviors that get you in trouble"). Simple prompts may be necessary, especially if the general range and type of behaviors are already known. For the Student-Directed Interview, only a listing of behaviors is requested. Operational definition of the behaviors should be left to the Functional Assessment Interview (FAI) intended for use with the adults who provide support.

Identify the contexts where problem behaviors occur Section III provides an opportunity to identify times and locations where problem behaviors are most likely. A Student Daily Schedule Matrix (see the example in Figure 2.3) is presented to the student and he or she is asked to mark or point to times, classes, or activities during which the problematic behaviors are observed. In addition, the student is asked to rate the difficulty of the context (that is, a time or activity that may generate the problem behavior) by marking on a scale of 1 (least difficult) to 6 (most difficult). Contexts rated at 4 or above are then targeted for a further interview.

Develop summary statements This section allows you to develop specific hypothesis statements for each distinct context or maintaining function of the behavior. You will develop these summary statement "pictures" with the student by asking structured questions about setting events, predictors, and maintaining consequences. Each of the summary statement components is described below.

Define what "sets up" and "sets off" the behavior. Besides defining the general contexts for problem behavior, you will ask questions about specific aspects of the situations in which the problem behaviors occur. Ask the student, "What important events tend to set up the behavior? What appears to set off the problem behavior?" You may mark *event or activity* variables such as predictability of the schedule or distractions, *curricular* variables such as task difficulty or limited choices, *social* variables such as teacher demands or peer teasing, and *setting* variables such as being tired, sick, or hungry. These variables often occasion problem behaviors. Learning about such relationships from the perspective of the student can be extremely helpful in determining the antecedents for his or her problem behavior.

One or more of these variables may be more powerful than others; for example, the behaviors may occur whenever a difficult task is presented, no matter who presents it or where it is presented. Keep in mind that combinations of predictor events are likely to be important as well. The problem behaviors may occur primarily during a particular class or activity, with a certain teacher, or while the student is working on a specific task.

Identify the outcomes/reinforcers maintaining the problem behaviors. Earlier you were obtaining information about the environmental variables that predict the occurrence of problem behavior. Here you learn how the behaviors "work" for the student. We assume that any behavior performed consistently results in some kind of desired outcome. There are two major types of outcomes or functions: to *obtain* something desirable or *escape* something undesirable. Being able to define the function of the behavior from the perspective of the student will help you build support strategies, such as teaching or promoting desirable behaviors that can replace the behaviors of concern.

Student Daily Schedule

Please place an "X" in each column to show the times and classes where you have difficulty with the behaviors we talked about. If you have a lot of difficulty during a period, place an "X" on or near the 6. If you have a little difficulty during the class or hall time, place the "X" on or near the 1. We can practice on a couple together before we start.

Subject, Teacher	Before School	1st Period	Hall	2nd Period	Hall	3rd Period	Hall	4th Period	Lunch	5th Period	Hall	6th Period	Hall	7th Period	Hall	8th Period	After School
	none	Math Horner	none	Science Wolf	none	Reading Welch	none	P.E. Egan	none	Social Studies Gibb	none	Shop Bix	none	Study Hall Misuka	none	NA	none
Most Difficult 6								X									
5						X								X			
4				X													
3		X								X							
2			X		X		X		X		X	X	X		X		
Least Difficult 1	X																

Figure 2.3 Example of Completed Daily Schedule Matrix (from Student-Directed Functional Assessment Interview)

Develop a diagram describing the problem behavior situations In this section, you should draw the diagram that outlines the problem behavior situations including (a) the relevant setting events, (b) the relevant predictors, (c) the problem behaviors, and (d) the consequences maintaining the behaviors. In addition, you should include the desired appropriate behaviors that the student should be exhibiting in the problem situation (such as doing assigned work or attending to the teacher's presentation) and one or more alternative behaviors that the student could perform to achieve the same outcome as the problem behaviors (for example, raise hand to request assistance/attention). Figure 2.4 presents an example of such a diagram. (Note: We will discuss such "competing behavior" diagrams in more detail in Chapter 3, which deals with the development of programmatic strategies based on assessment information.)

Identify important features of a support plan and potential alternative behaviors In this section you should briefly list the programming strategies you have identified relevant to each of the different categories (see the example in Figure 2.5). Completing the form helps you see how the different strategies will work to prevent and/or remediate the problem situations by attacking them from different perspectives. The interview solicits suggestions from the student regarding changes that would promote appropriate behaviors and decrease the likelihood of problem behaviors. The student can be prompted to identify *ways to change the context* (such as reconfigure class layouts, take more time to complete assignments, get more sleep at night, eat a good breakfast), *ways to prevent the problem behaviors* (shorter tasks, more help from the teacher), *ways to increase expected behavior or teach a replacement behavior* (such as practicing the replacement behavior), *what should happen*

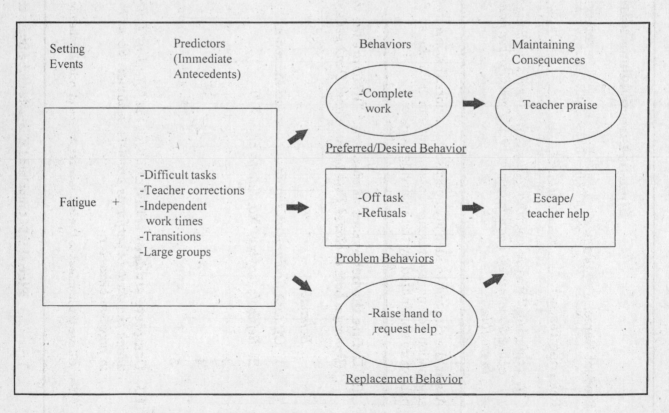

Figure 2.4 Summary Diagram of Problem Behavior Situation

Student-Directed Functional Assessment Interview

Student Name: _____James_____   Interviewer: _____Jane S._____

Referring Teacher: _____Ms. Rodriguez_____   Date: _____2-16-96_____

I. **Opening.** *"We are meeting today to find ways to change school so that you like it more. This interview will take about 30 minutes. I can help you best if you answer honestly. You will not be asked anything that might get you in trouble."*

Assist the student to identify specific behaviors that are resulting in problems in the school or classroom. Making suggestions or paraphrasing statements can help the student clarify his or her ideas. You should have a list of behaviors nominated by the referring teacher.

II. **Define the behaviors of concern.** * *"What are the things you do that get you in trouble or are a problem?"* (Prompts: *Late to class? Talk out in class? Don't get work done? Fighting?*)

Behavior   *Comment*

1. *Off task (looking and walking around the room)*

2. *Refusals (saying "No, I don't have to")*

3.

4.

5.

III. **Complete student schedule.** *Use the "Student Daily Schedule" matrix to identify the times and classes in which the student performs problem behavior. Focus the interview on those times that are **most likely** to result in problem behavior.*

* You will use the numbers to the left as codes for the identified behaviors as you complete the rest of the interview.

Figure 2.5 Completed Example of the Student-Directed Functional Assessment Interview

Student Daily Schedule

Please place an "X" in each column to show the times and classes where you have difficulty with the behaviors we talked about. If you have a lot of difficulty during a period, place an "X" on or near the 6. If you have a little difficulty during the class or hall time, place the "X" on or near the 1. We can practice on a couple together before we start.

Subject, Teacher	Before School none	1st Period Reading Hall	Hall none	2nd Period Math Jones	Hall none	3rd Period Science Elliot	Hall none	4th Period P.E. Bendix	Lunch none	5th Period Social Studies Smith	Hall none	6th Period Music Best	Hall none	7th Period Study Hall Ozan	Hall none	8th Period Special Matthew	After School none
Most Difficult 6				X													
5		X								X						X	
4			X		X		X	X	X		X	X	X				
3						X						X	X	X	X		
2																	
Least Difficult 1	X																X

Figure 2.5 (*continued*)

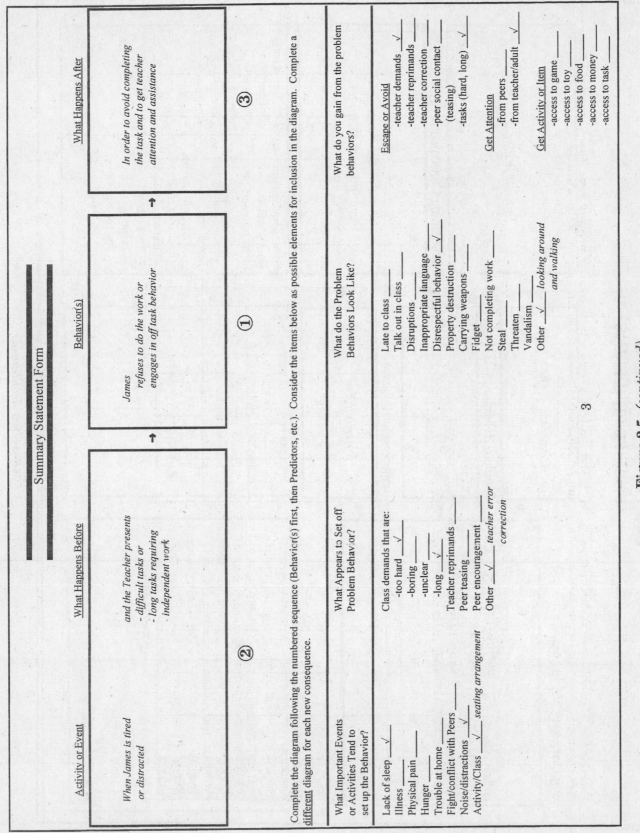

Summary Statement Form

Activity or Event

②

When James is tired or distracted

What Happens Before

and the Teacher presents
- difficult tasks or
- long tasks requiring
* independent work*

Behavior(s)

①

James
refuses to do the work or
engages in off task behavior

What Happens After

③

In order to avoid completing the task and to get teacher attention and assistance

Complete the diagram following the numbered sequence (Behavior(s) first, then Predictors, etc.). Consider the items below as possible elements for inclusion in the diagram. Complete a <u>different diagram</u> for each new consequence.

What Important Events or Activities Tend to set up the Behavior?

Lack of sleep   √
Illness _____
Physical pain _____
Hunger _____
Trouble at home _____
Fight/conflict with Peers _____
Noise/distractions   √
Activity/Class   √   *seating arrangement*

What Appears to Set off Problem Behavior?

Class demands that are:
  -too hard   √
  -boring _____
  -unclear _____
  -long   √
Teacher reprimands _____
Peer teasing _____
Peer encouragement _____
Other   √   *teacher error correction*

What do the Problem Behaviors Look Like?

Late to class _____
Talk out in class _____
Disruptions _____
Inappropriate language _____
Disrespectful behavior   √
Property destruction _____
Carrying weapons _____
Fidget _____
Not completing work _____
Steal _____
Threaten _____
Vandalism _____
Other   √   *looking around and walking*

What do you gain from the problem behaviors?

Escape or Avoid
  -teacher demands   √
  -teacher reprimands _____
  -teacher correction _____
  -peer social contact _____
   (teasing)
  -tasks (hard, long)   √

Get Attention
  -from peers _____
  -from teacher/adult   √

Get Activity or Item
  -access to game _____
  -access to toy _____
  -access to food _____
  -access to money _____
  -access to task _____

3

Figure 2.5 *(continued)*

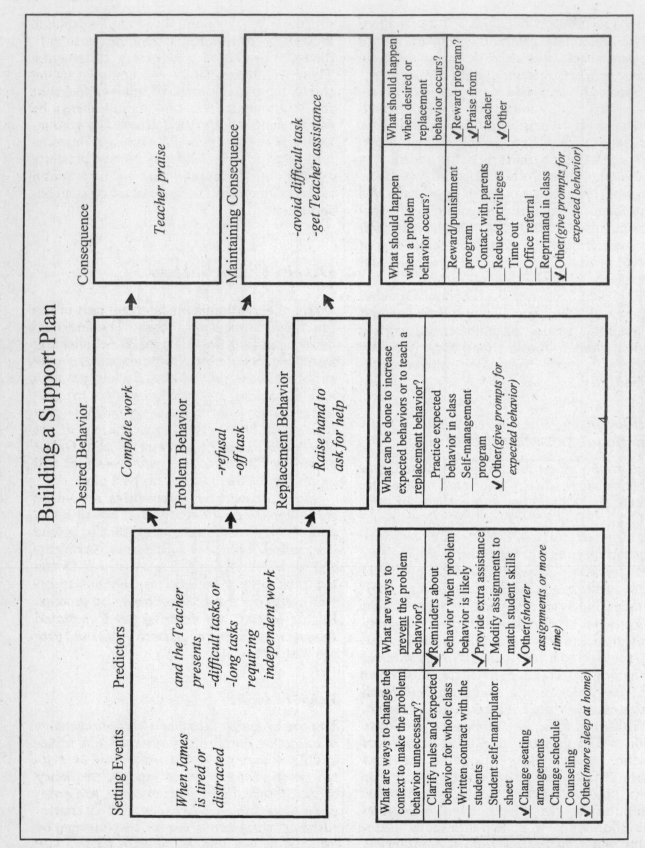

Building a Support Plan

Setting Events

When James is tired or distracted

Predictors

and the Teacher presents
-difficult tasks or
-long tasks requiring independent work

Desired Behavior

Complete work

Problem Behavior

-refusal
-off task

Replacement Behavior

Raise hand to ask for help

Consequence

Teacher praise

Maintaining Consequence

-avoid difficult task
-get Teacher assistance

What are ways to change the context to make the problem behavior unnecessary?
___ Clarify rules and expected behavior for whole class
___ Written contract with the students
___ Student self-manipulator sheet
✔ Change seating arrangements
___ Change schedule
___ Counseling
✔ Other *(more sleep at home)*

What are ways to prevent the problem behavior?
✔ Reminders about behavior when problem behavior is likely
✔ Provide extra assistance
___ Modify assignments to match student skills
✔ Other *(shorter assignments or more time)*

What can be done to increase expected behaviors or to teach a replacement behavior?
___ Practice expected behavior in class
___ Self-management program
✔ Other *(give prompts for expected behavior)*

What should happen when a problem behavior occurs?
___ Reward/punishment program
___ Contact with parents
___ Reduced privileges
___ Time out
___ Office referral
___ Reprimand in class
✔ Other *(give prompts for expected behavior)*

What should happen when desired or replacement behavior occurs?
✔ Reward program?
✔ Praise from teacher
✔ Other

Figure 2.5 *(continued)*

when the problem behavior occurs (reduced privileges, office referral), or *what should happen when the desired or replacement behavior occurs* (praise or special rewards).

Students can use communicative responses as replacements for problem behaviors, such as raising a hand and asking for assistance rather than talking out and throwing or destroying materials. In addition, a student may have other behaviors in his or her repertoire that can serve as alternatives to problem behaviors. For example, if a student makes loud noises to gain the attention of his or her peers, you could teach her or him to wait until an assignment is completed and then approach a peer for interaction.

Figure 2.5 presents a Student-Directed Functional Assessment Interview completed by a middle school teacher working with a student named James. Read the interview, keeping in mind the major outcomes described earlier.

Validating the Student-Directed Functional Assessment Interview

Once an interview has been completed, you will have a great deal of information about the student and his or her suggestions for support. After the interview data are collected and summarized, you will need to compare information from relevant adults and the student. You may find that different respondents do not agree on all the details regarding environment, behavior functions, or support plan suggestions. If there is substantial disagreement, direct observation data collection can help to resolve the confusion. We recommend confirming information from the interviews with observational data no matter how much agreement exists between adults and the student.

Whatever types of interviews you have conducted, you must decide at this point whether you should continue to the next stages of information gathering: systematic direct observation and possibly systematic manipulations. This decision will depend on your confidence with the summary statements you constructed from the interview

process. We have found that complex problem behaviors require direct observation to validate the preliminary summary statements. There is no substitute for actually seeing things happen. Because of this, we feel that the interview information should always be supplemented with data gathered by systematic direct observation. (Remember Outcome 5 in Box 1.1.) The following section presents a form and procedures that we have found efficient and effective for conducting such observations.

Direct Observation

Direct observation is an essential part of the functional assessment process. The final outcome identified for this process is collecting direct observation data to validate and clarify summary statements about what predicts and maintains problem behaviors. In situations where informant methods fail to provide clear and helpful information, direct observation data will serve as the basis for the summary statements or hypotheses that will guide development of the support plan.

Direct observation procedures should be structured to provide clear and useful information while not overburdening the people responsible for collecting the data. Our strategy for accomplishing this balance is to use the results of functional assessment interviews to guide the direct observation process. In this section, we describe the Functional Assessment Observation form (FAO) and procedures for its use.

Keep It Simple

You are probably familiar with various ways of collecting data on the occurrence of undesirable behaviors, such as anecdotal or written descriptions, incident reports, frequency counts, interval recording systems, and antecedent-behavior-consequence (A-B-C) charts. Although these can be useful, they also can be difficult to use and summarize easily. The

FAO and procedures described below are designed around a straightforward event recording procedure, in which entries are made on the recording form only when an incident involving the targeted behavior occurs. The form is structured to maximize the comprehensive information that you can obtain without going through lengthy writeups or summarizing, as with written anecdotal descriptions. The form also allows for monitoring patterns of behavior over long time periods.

When and Where Should Observations Be Done?

Use the FAO to collect data across as many settings and as much time per day as possible. Separate copies of the form can be used across multiple settings—one for school, one for home, one for work—or a single copy can accompany a person from setting to setting. When a form is used within a particular setting, collect data across all times when the person is in that setting. Gathering information across as many different settings and times of day as possible is important. Using such a broad database will help you identify where and when problem behaviors both *do* and *do not* occur.

The FAO form is designed for use in monitoring behaviors that occur at a low to moderate frequency (fewer than 20 times per day). For such behaviors, observations and data recording can occur across extended periods without interfering with the ongoing job performance of support providers. When problem behaviors or behavioral incidents occur with higher frequency, the form requires modification. Rather than trying to record after every incident throughout the day, and by that overburdening support staff with data collection responsibilities, a time sampling approach should be used. Data should be recorded only during particular, shorter periods, such as during one 15-minute block in a one-hour period. An additional support person, if available, may be used during the time sample to observe and record data. With high-frequency behaviors, ample opportunities to observe targeted behaviors are likely to occur

within short times. These time samples can be spread throughout a day and across settings to provide a clear picture of behavior patterns. Introductory textbooks in behavioral support provide specific examples of how to observe more frequent problem behaviors (cf. Wolery, Bailey, & Sugai, 1988, in Appendix A).

Who Should Observe?

Observation data should be collected by people directly in contact with the person with problem behaviors, such as teachers, residential and work support providers, and parents and family members. If several people are recording data, be sure that each is familiar with the guidelines and procedures for data collection. Some initial training and occasional ongoing support for troubleshooting are necessary for people to become comfortable collecting data with the FAO. To avoid problems and confusion in situations where multiple support providers are present, such as in a school classroom, designate one person to be responsible for recording on the form during a particular time period (a school period, one day, one week). Staff in schools, workplaces, and homes can generally be trained to collect FAO data accurately in a 45-minute training session.

How Long Should Direct Observation Data Be Collected?

Ideally, observation data should be collected until clear patterns have emerged with regard to relationships between behaviors and environmental situations and events, and statements regarding the potential functions of behaviors have been confirmed or unconfirmed. Typically, to reach this point will require a minimum of 15 to 20 occurrences of the targeted behaviors. We recommend that data be collected for a minimum of 2 to 5 days; however, the frequency with which behaviors occur will affect the length of time that observation data must be collected. Whether data collection is needed beyond an initial 2- to 5-day period will depend on the consistency and clarity of the behavior-environment relationships observed.

In considering how long to collect direct observation data, it is important to recognize that behaviors and environmental conditions change over time. Functional assessment is not a one-shot process. It may be useful within the behavioral support process to include procedures for periodic or even ongoing collection of direct observation functional assessment data. We know of many situations in which the FAO or a variation of it has been used as the regular ongoing data collection procedure within a setting.

What Does the Functional Assessment Observation Form Do?

The FAO documents the predictor events and consequences associated with instances of problem behavior. The form is organized around *problem behavior events*. An *event* is different from a single occurrence of a problem behavior. An event includes *all* the problem behaviors in an incident that begins with a problem behavior and ends only after 3 minutes of no problem behavior. In this way, a problem behavior event could be (a) an incident with a single, brief scream; (b) an incident lasting 5 minutes, with continuous screaming; or (c) an incident lasting 10 minutes involving several problem behaviors, each performed multiple times. Counting *events* is easier, more accurate, and more informative than trying to count the exact frequency (as with head hits) or duration (as with screams) of problem behaviors.

The FAO indicates (a) the number of events of problem behavior, (b) the problem behaviors that occur together, (c) the times when problem behavior events are most and least likely to occur, (d) events that predict problem behavior events, (e) perceptions about the maintaining function of problem behaviors, and (f) actual consequences following problem behavior events. Together these pieces of information have been useful in validating and clarifying summary statements. In most cases we find that the information

from an FAO provides enough information to allow us to move confidently into development of behavior support plans.

The Content of the Functional Assessment Observation Form

The FAO has eight major sections (see Figure 2.6). A blank copy of the form is included in Appendix D. Each labeled section is described below.

Section A: Identification/dates In Section A, you show who is being observed and the dates on which the data are being collected. Note that a single page can be used across multiple days.

Section B: Time intervals Section B is separated into blocks that can be used to designate specific intervals (1 hour, a half-hour, 15 minutes). List here the periods and settings/activities in which observation is taking place. These can be arranged in a variety of ways, depending on a person's daily schedule. For a school student you might list class period times and content (for example, 8:30–9:00, Homeroom; 9:05–9:50, Language Arts; 9:55–10:40, Computer; 11:45–12:30, Lunch; 1:25–3:00, Job Training). For an adult in a less structured home setting, you might simply list time periods (3:00–4:00; 4:00–5:00; 5:00–6:00). Depending on a person's typical pattern of behavior or typical schedule, you may want to use unequal interval sizes within the blocks, such as 15-minute intervals during busy morning routines and 2-hour intervals during the evening when problem behaviors are much less frequent. If targeted behaviors are very frequent during a particular time period or activity, multiple blocks can be used to record data for that period. A row for summarizing total frequencies of behaviors or incidents is labeled at the bottom of the form.

Section C: Behaviors In Section C, list the individual behaviors you have identified for monitoring during the observations. These targeted behaviors should be the ones identified during your interviews with relevant peo-

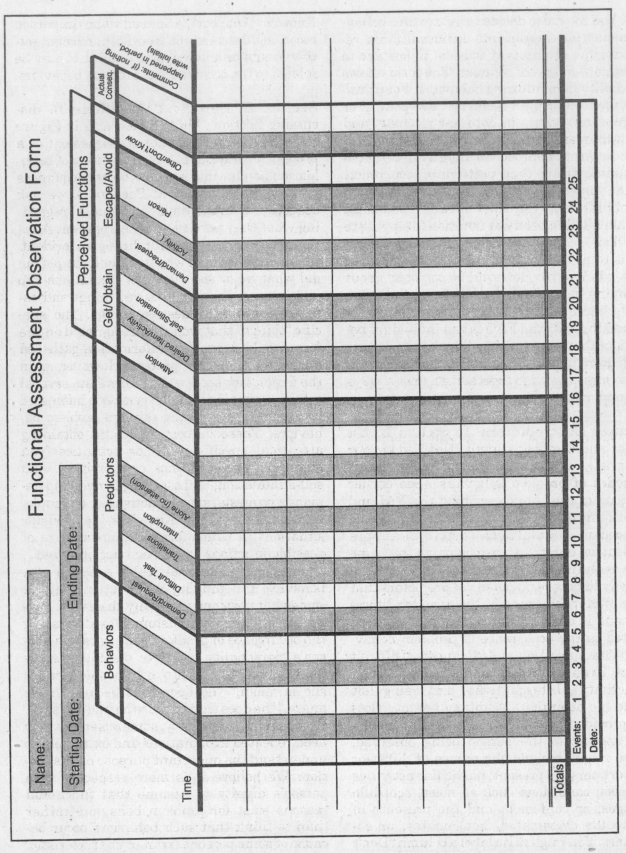

Figure 2.6   Functional Assessment Observation Form

ple. You may also decide to list *positive* behaviors such as appropriate communication responses or attempts that seem important to document or are of interest. The form allows flexibility in monitoring behaviors. For example, if a particular behavior (eye-poking or aggression) occurs in both low-intensity and high-intensity forms, you can list each form as a separate behavior to identify differences or similarities in their patterns of occurrence. When several behaviors occur regularly in combinations, you may monitor them all within a single behavior notation (dropping to the floor, screaming, kicking feet and flailing arms to pound the floor may all be recorded under tantrum). However, be cautious about grouping behaviors together for coding. One of the more useful pieces of information obtained through the FAO is the individual behaviors that tend to occur together and those that do not. Initial perceptions that certain behaviors always go together may not always be supported by direct observation data.

Section D: Predictors In Section D, list important events or stimuli identified in your interviews as potential predictors for the occurrence of problem behaviors. (See earlier sections of the book describing the FAI and identifying general setting events and specific antecedent stimuli.) Such events typically are present or occur just before or at the same time as the problem behaviors. The FAO form already lists several potential predictors that have often been found in the research literature and in our own clinical experiences to be related to the occurrence of problem behaviors. These are Demands/Requests, Difficult Tasks, Transitions (place to place or activity to activity), Interruptions, and being left Alone (no attention). Additional empty slots are provided for you to list potential predictors specific to the person being observed. These might include the names of different support persons present; particular activities or tasks; conditions such as noise, schedule changes, or confusion; and the presence of particular classmates, housemates, or coworkers. You might also label a column "Don't

Know" or "Unclear" to be used when the person recording data cannot identify particular setting events or antecedent stimuli that may be related to the occurrence of problem behaviors.

Section E: Perceived functions In discussing Section D of the FAI, and in Figure 2.1, we presented functional assessment as a process for identifying the functions of problem behaviors in terms of the consequences that maintain them. In Section E, we ask observers to make their "best guess" regarding what they perceive as the apparent function of behaviors that occur during an incident. In other words, note why you think the person did what he or she did. This section has two major areas: obtaining desired things and escaping/avoiding undesired things. The specific "things" that would be designated on the form would depend on information gathered during the interview process. However, as in the Predictors section, the form lists several outcomes that individuals have been interested in obtaining or escaping through problem behaviors. These outcomes include obtaining attention, specific items or activities (you might list specific items or activities), and self-stimulation; and escaping or avoiding demands/requests, specific activities, or people. A column for "Don't Know" is included for situations in which observers are unsure of possible functions of the behavior observed.

Focusing on the particular outcome of a behavior and judging its function may be somewhat new ideas for many observers. People are often more accustomed to attributing the occurrence of problem behaviors to a person's "personality traits" or disability labels (for example, "she likes to hurt people because she is mean," "he does that because he is angry," "he does that because he has autism"). Because of this tendency, some observers may need repeated explanations and extra help to understand the important purpose of this section. We believe it is more respectful of a person's dignity to assume that functional reasons exist for problem behaviors rather than to think that such behaviors occur because of some personal trait or characteristic.

Section F: Actual consequences In Section F, you record data on the actual consequences that follow problem behaviors—for example, the person was told "no," was put in a time-out area, was ignored, was redirected. This information gives you some idea of the consistency with which certain consequences are being provided. It also provides further clues to the potential functions of problem behaviors. For instance, if a time-out procedure is being implemented with problem behaviors that appear to be escape motivated, then putting the student in a time-out area may actually be reinforcing the behaviors.

Section G: Comments Observers can write brief comments here regarding behaviors that occurred during the corresponding block of time. We also recommend that observers use this space to write their initials for a block of time in which no targeted behaviors were observed. This practice verifies that observation was occurring and that no problem behaviors were observed. As we noted earlier, knowing when and under what circumstances problem behaviors do *not* occur can be very informative.

Section H: Event and date record The rows of numbers in Section H are designed to help the observer keep track of the number of problem behavior events that have occurred and the days across which these events were observed. The numbers are used to show each event with one or more problem behaviors.

The first time a behavior or incident occurs, the data recorder should mark the appropriate boxes on the form with the number 1 to identify the first recorded event of the behavior. The number 1 in the Events row of Section H would then be crossed off. The next occurrence of problem behaviors and the relevant boxes in each section of the form would be recorded by using the next number in the row (2 indicates the second occurrence, 3 indicates the third, and so on). Each time a number is used, it is crossed off. When recording is finished on a particular day, a slash can be drawn after the last number and the day's date recorded in the Date row below to indicate the date on which those incidents occurred. During the next day's data collection, the first incident would be recorded using the next unused number in the row (such as 5 or 6) and would then continue with the following numbers (7, 8, 9, 10). Using numbers in this way for each incident or occurrence of targeted behaviors enables you to link specific predictors, functions, and consequences with behaviors. If the same data sheet is used across multiple days, notations in the Date row help you see which incidents occurred on which days. Such information can be helpful as you look for patterns across time or try to validate what people tell you about the way a person's behaviors may vary on particular days (for example, "Her behavior is always worst on Mondays"). The steps for setting up the FAO to collect data are summarized in Box 2.2. Figure 2.7 shows a form on which

---

BOX 2.2 Steps for Setting Up a Functional Assessment Observation Form for Collecting Data

1. Write basic identifying information and dates of observations.
2. List the time intervals and settings/activities down the left side of the form.
3. List the behaviors to be monitored.
4. List potentially relevant setting events and/or more immediate antecedent events in the Predictors section.
5. List any additional possible functions of behaviors, if necessary, in the Perceived Functions section.
6. List the actual consequences that are typically delivered when behaviors occur.

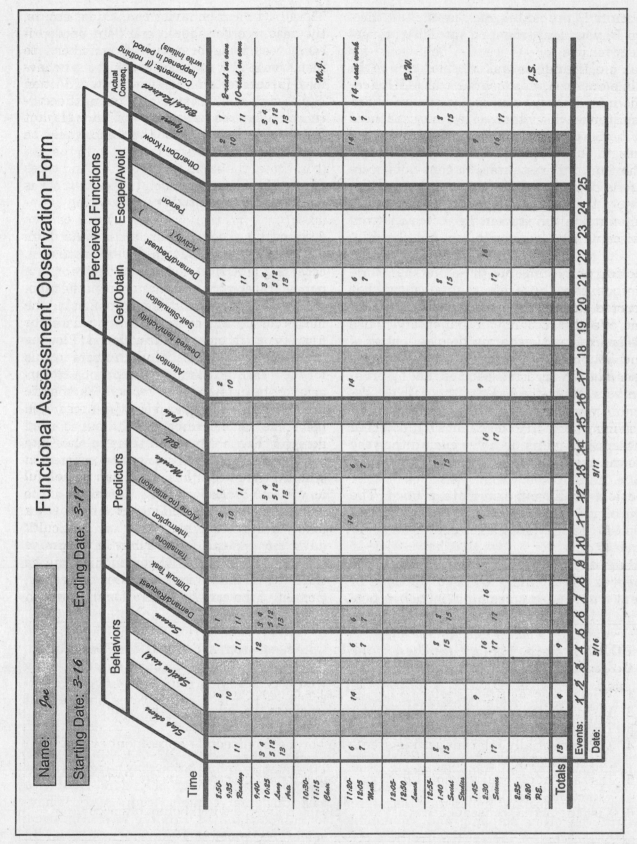

Figure 2.7 Completed Observation Form for Joe

behaviors, predictors, perceived functions, and actual consequences are filled in and ready for use.

A quick analysis and interpretation of the data presented in the completed FAO (Figure 2.7) reveal several pieces of important information. Joe was observed for 2 days (3/16 and 3/17) during which a total of 17 events of problem behavior were coded (see Events row at bottom). Three problem behaviors were observed: slapping others, spitting on the desk, and screaming. Predictors added to the form for monitoring were the three classroom assistants who work with Joe: Marsha, Bill, and John. Actual consequences to Joe were blocking and redirection or having the behavior ignored. The Time column shows the school periods and times during which data were collected.

The observation data show clear patterns in the occurrence of problem behaviors. Look at the very first event involving problem behaviors. It is coded with a 1. This first event included both slapping others and screaming (a 1 in both columns). It occurred when a demand/request was made during the reading period (1's are in the row for 8:50 to 9:35). Marsha was working with Joe (see a 1 under Marsha for the period) and she implemented a block/redirect procedure. The perceived function was escape from the demand/request.

In looking for overall patterns, we see that slapping others (which occurred 12 times in the two days) and screaming (9 occurrences) frequently occurred together—but not always (see events 3, 4, and 5). This finding suggests that these two behaviors are members of the same response class and are used for the same function. The perceived function for both behaviors is escape from demands/requests. Note that screaming did occur once by itself during Science on 3/17 (see the event coded with 16). The predictor was a difficult task and the perceived function was escape from the task. This particular screaming incident was ignored. Blocking and redirection were used in the other slapping and screaming events. Spitting on the desk, which was ob-

served four times, was seen as serving an attention-getting function. The predictor noted was that Joe was working alone (no attention). The comments column provides even further information for events 2, 10, and 14. Despite the perceived function, the spitting was ignored by school staff, at least during the observation period presented here.

Using the Functional Assessment Observation Form

Recording The basic use of the FAO form is straightforward. Recording is event driven, occurring whenever a problem behavior or a behavioral episode or incident involving problem behaviors occurs. When problem behaviors occur during a time interval, place the appropriate number from Section H (1 for the first occurrence or episode, 2 for the second, 3 for the third, and so on) in the appropriate box or boxes in the Behaviors section. Then move horizontally across the rest of the form and place the same number in the appropriate boxes in the other sections, thereby recording the Predictors (setting events and antecedent stimuli) that were present when the behaviors occurred, the Perceived Functions of the behaviors, and the Actual Consequences that followed the occurrence of the behaviors. Finally, cross off the number used in Section H so you can easily see which number will be used next. If a comment is needed or desired, write it in the corresponding Comments box. Also, to facilitate follow-up on observations, observers could write their initials in the Comments box at the end of a time period, particularly if there is no other way to identify who was observing during a period. The example in Figure 2.7 illustrates how several occurrences of problem behaviors might be recorded.

When problem behaviors occur relatively infrequently, information may be recorded for each occurrence of the behaviors. In such a case, an actual frequency count of the behavior can be obtained from the form. However, sometimes problem behaviors will occur in high-frequency bursts (such as several head hits or face slaps in rapid succession), or in episodes that include multiple occurrences of one or more problem behaviors (such as a 5-minute tantrum that involves dropping to the floor, kicking feet, screaming, several hits, and attempted bites). In such cases observers should code the entire burst or episode with a single entry on the form—that is, one number representing the entire episode or burst. Using this method, the frequency of bursts or episodes can be determined but not the actual frequency of each problem behavior.

Finally, for behaviors that occur with high frequency, the form should be used for brief time sample periods in which only a few, or even just one, occurrence or incident is recorded. This approach greatly reduces demands related to data collection but may also result in information being missed. The hope in such a case would be that high frequency behaviors occur so often that a clear picture will emerge even if all occurrences are not recorded.

No matter the recording approach used, support personnel and observers should ensure that the health, safety, and support needs of a person engaging in problem behaviors are met before they shift their attention to recording information on the observation form. *Data collection should not interfere with the delivery of needed support or intervention.* However, the person responsible for collecting data should record information when possible following the occurrence of problem behaviors to ensure accuracy and guard against the loss of information. The copy of the FAO form that is being used for data collection should be located in a convenient, central place where those responsible for observation have ready access for recording, such as on a clipboard or in a file on the teacher's desk.

As noted earlier, knowing where and when problem behaviors are *not* occurring can be very useful. If no problem behaviors occur during a time period, we recommend that the observer write his or her initials in the appropriate Comments column box to indicate that observation was occurring during this period. This eliminates the question of whether the absence of data during a period means that no problem behavior occurred or nobody was observing at that time. Having observers include their initials also allows you to know who was observing during a given time period in case you want to follow up on what was happening during the period. Box 2.3 summarizes the basic steps in the recording process.

Initial training People who will be using the FAO form need to be trained before using

---

BOX 2.3 Basic Steps for Recording Data on the Functional Assessment Observation Form

1. If problem behaviors occur during a recording interval:
   a. Recorder puts first unused number (from bottom list, Section H) in appropriate box or boxes in Behaviors section.
   b. Recorder uses the same number to mark appropriate boxes in the Predictors, Perceived Functions, and Actual Consequences sections.
   c. Recorder crosses out just-used number in the list at the bottom of the form.
   d. Recorder writes any desired comments in the Comments column.
   e. At the end of the time period the recorder puts his or her initials in the Comments box.
2. If problem behaviors do *not* occur during a recording interval:
   a. Recorder puts his or her initials in the Comments box for that interval and writes any desired comments.

the form independently. Training should involve describing the different sections of the form and how they are used, and providing practice on recording on the form before actual observation begins. We provide a practice exercise in the following section of this handbook. Training also should include specific information on the logistics of the observation and recording processes to be used. This includes writing on the form the actual time intervals to be employed, identifying the persons responsible for recording data, specifying where the form will be located and stored, and determining the planned schedule for observations. Once actual observation has begun, someone in a supervisory or monitoring capacity should discuss with the observers any issues or problems that arise. It is not unusual to need to revise the observation form or procedures after a day or two of actual recording. For example, behaviors or predictors may occur that were overlooked in the initial interviews and form setup and will need to be added to the form. Behaviors or predictors (difficult tasks, transitions) may need to be more clearly defined for consistent recording. Procedures (such as where the form is kept) may need to be modified.

Exercise in Form Setup, Observation, and Recording

This section presents the following: (a) descriptive information about an individual (Yolanda Martin) who engages in problem behavior, (b) some information that would be derived from an interview for setting up an FAO, and (c) a description of a series of behavioral incidents. Your task in this exercise is first to set up the blank FAO form presented in Figure 2.8 with the relevant information (name, dates, behaviors, predictors, actual consequences, and so on). Then read each description of a behavioral incident and record its occurrence on the form, using appropriate numbers and marking appropriate boxes.

Basic information Yolanda Martin is 8 years old. She currently attends a regular

third-grade class and has been labeled as having behavior disorders according to state and school district guidelines. She can do some grade level work in reading and language arts but does more poorly in mathematics and other subjects. She is willing to interact, at least briefly, with most of her peers in the class, but there are two or three peers who are reported to "set her off." In recent months Yolanda has been exhibiting ever more disruptive behavior, including verbally refusing to do things when requested, bothering peers during work times, yelling, destroying work materials, and trying to hit or kick the teacher and other students. These behaviors are causing significant concerns for Yolanda's parents and her teachers.

Yolanda is going to be observed over the course of 3 school days (Jan. 30 to Feb. 1). Her typical schedule includes the following:

8:15–8:45	Opening/Planning and silent reading period
8:45–9:45	Reading/Language Arts groups
9:45–10:45	Science/Social Studies (whole class/small groups)
10:45–11:45	Math period (groups, independent work)
11:45–12:30	Lunch and recess
12:30–1:30	Story reading group
1:30–2:30	Independent seat work period
2:30–3:15	Art projects

Based on a functional assessment interview, Yolanda's primary behaviors of concern include yelling, destroying materials, and hitting/kicking the teacher and her peers. Some particular predictors identified as important include proximity to "problem peers" and being in math group. The actual consequences that are supposed to be provided for her behaviors include verbal redirection and being sent to sit in the corner. *At this point you should complete the basic identifying information and set up the other sections of the form.*

Behavioral incidents Each of the following descriptions identifies the time of day a behavioral incident occurred, what behaviors were seen, what predictors were observed,

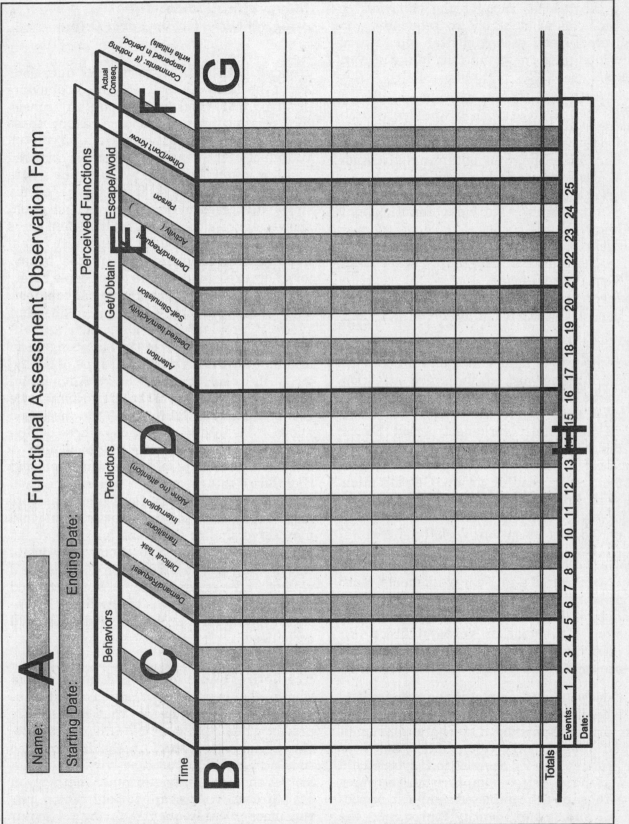

Figure 2.8 Blank Observation Form for Exercise

why the teacher thought the behaviors occurred, and what actual consequences were delivered. Read each vignette, and then record it on the form by marking in the relevant boxes.

Jan. 30

Incident 1. 8:34 a.m. Yolanda yelled out loudly. No one was talking or working with her. Function was obtaining attention. Verbally redirected to activity.

Incident 2. 9:50 a.m. Kicked peer on leg. Social Studies group. No clear function/don't know. Sent to corner.

Incident 3. 11:15 a.m. Tear book and slap teacher's arm. Math group. Escape tasks. Verbally redirected.

Incident 4. 2:11 p.m. Yelled out. Seat work period. Get attention. Ignored.

Jan. 31

Incident 5. 8:40 a.m. Yelled and hit peer. No one talking/working with. Get attention. Verbal redirect and sent to corner.

Incident 6. 10:48 a.m. Yelled and swept books off desk. Math worksheet period. Escape tasks. Verbal redirect.

Incident 7. 12:45 p.m. Stepped on teacher's foot. Story reading group. Get attention. Verbal redirect.

Incident 8. 1:42 p.m. Yelled out. Seat work period. Get attention. Verbal redirect.

Feb. 1

Incident 9. 11:40 a.m. Tear worksheets. Math group. Escape tasks. Verbal redirect.

Incident 10. 12:15 p.m. Hit peer. Playing alone. Get attention. Verbal redirect.

Incident 11. 2:45 p.m. Yelled out. Silent art project. Get attention. Verbal redirect.

Once you have completed the exercise (and only then!), you can compare your results with the form in Appendix E. If there are significant discrepancies between this example form and your completed exercise form, you should reread the vignettes, compare your responses with those on the completed sample in Appendix E, and try to identify and correct the errors you have made.

Interpreting Functional Analysis Observation Form Data

Describing behaviors Initial questions about the data seek to detect *which* behaviors occurred and whether there are any consistent relationships or patterns among these problem behaviors. Observation data can tell you which of the identified behaviors occurred and how often. For example, Yolanda's data indicate that across 3 days, she yelled six times, destroyed materials three times, and showed aggression toward teachers and peers a total of five times. Such data can also reveal important relationships among the behaviors. Our experience shows that people rarely engage in only one type of problem behavior. They more commonly engage in different types of problem behaviors, such as self-injury and aggression, or they may engage in different forms of a particular type of behavior, such as self-injurious head banging and hand biting. Certain behaviors may be grouped together into a class (as discussed above in the interview section). These behaviors usually occur close together in some type of sequence. A person may always yell and then throw things, or begin rocking and then start hand biting. Such classes of behaviors may be related to similar predictor events and may serve similar functions for individuals. For example, the data for Yolanda indicate that yelling and destroying materials, and yelling and aggression sometimes occurred together as Yolanda was trying to get attention or escape from nonpreferred tasks and activities.

Predicting behaviors Observational data should also provide information about situational aspects and events that consistently predict when behaviors *will* and *will not* occur. A first major aspect to consider would be time periods and related activities. You can look at the data and determine whether you see patterns with regard to behaviors occurring more or less frequently during particular periods and activities. The data should also provide information on more specific events or antecedents that appear consistently related to behavior. These might include the "standard" events included on the form (such as Demands/Requests) and additional ones added based on interviews (the "Problem Peers" were added for Yolanda).

Again, Yolanda's data provide an example. Seat work periods and other activities with little attention may be consistently related to the occurrence of yelling. Being asked to do apparently nonpreferred math tasks was consistently related to the destruction of materials and once to aggression. Other periods appeared relatively problem free (such as Reading/Language Arts). The data make it possible to identify both consistent time periods, activities, and events that are predictive of the occurrence and nonoccurrence of problem behavior.

Determining the functions of behaviors (maintaining outcomes/reinforcers)

Learning about the reinforcers that maintain behaviors is a key element in being able to use assessment information for developing programming and support strategies. For example, if someone is engaging in self-injurious or aggressive behaviors to access tangible items or objects, considering a variety of interventions would be possible. The person could be taught more appropriate alternative ways of achieving the same outcome (that is, appropriate communicative requests). In addition, the desired items could be used as contingent reinforcers for appropriate behavior and could also be provided frequently on a noncontingent basis to reduce the occasions for problem behaviors.

The sections of the form dealing with perceived functions and actual consequences can supply the most direct information about potential functions and maintaining reinforcers. Again, Yolanda's data provide an example. In the Perceived Functions section, observers showed that her behaviors were serving two primary functions: (a) gaining attention and (b) escaping requests to complete nonpreferred tasks. Looking at the actual consequences provided is also of interest. On a number of occasions when the perceived

function was to gain attention, Yolanda was verbally redirected back to the activity. This redirection may be serving as a form of reinforcing attention for such behavior and would need to be considered when intervention strategies are planned.

Yolanda's data illustrate a very important issue. Just as the research literature and our experience show that people rarely engage in only a single kind of problem behavior, they also indicate that many people often engage in problem behavior for different reasons at different times. That is, problem behavior can serve multiple functions for people. They may sometimes appear to use the same behavior to obtain different types of reinforcing outcomes, such as screaming both to get attention and to avoid undesirable activities. Other persons may appear to use different behaviors to obtain different reinforcers, such as screaming for attention and hitting and kicking to escape nonpreferred demands. A number of different types of such patterns can be identified. The critical issue is that we develop a detailed and complete picture of the patterns that exist for particular individuals to be sure that we develop and carry out programmatic strategies that will address all the relevant aspects of their behaviors and related maintaining reinforcers.

Confirming or Revising Initial Summary Statements

It is important to keep the overall view in mind when you look at the observation data. It is important to pay attention to specific sections of the form, but it is also critical to be looking for consistent overall patterns of behaviors, predictors, and perceived functions that might be occurring. One primary purpose of collecting observation data is to allow us to confirm, disconfirm, revise, or add to the initial summary statements we have developed based on interview and informant information. Once you have collected and analyzed enough data, you can then decide whether your initial ideas about different situations, behaviors, and maintaining reinforcers were accurate, or need to be revised. For example,

---

BOX 2.4 Basic Guidelines for Interpreting Data from the Functional Assessment Observation Form

Guideline 1: Examine the Behaviors columns to decide which behaviors are occurring, how often they are occurring, and whether some or all of the behaviors seem to be co-occurring regularly.

Guideline 2: Examine the form to see whether behaviors are consistently occurring during particular time periods and whether particular Predictors are consistently related to the occurrence of particular behaviors during those time periods.

Guideline 3: Consider the Perceived Functions and Actual Consequences sections of the form to identify the probable functions of different behaviors and the consequences that may be maintaining them.

Guideline 4: Based on the observation data, decide whether your initial summary statements seem valid, whether they should be revised or discarded, and whether you need to develop additional statements.

---

direct observation information will sometimes indicate that certain behaviors are not occurring in the ways that people had reported. Or observation may reveal additional behaviors and situations that need to be considered but that had not been clearly identified by informants. This clarification process will be an important step in moving to the selection and implementation of programmatic strategies. Box 2.4 presents basic guidelines for looking at and interpreting data collected with the FAO form.

Examples in Analyzing Data from Direct Observations

In this section we present more examples of data gathered from direct observations to provide you with practice in looking at and interpreting data, and developing summary statements.

Example 1: Erin The first example, shown in Figure 2.9, provides data for Erin in her work setting. This example is relatively straightforward. After looking at Erin's data, take a few minutes to think about a summary statement based on the data. Write this statement in the following box, in the space marked "Summary Statements for Erin."

Once you have done this (and only then!) you can look at the list of summary statements presented in Appendix F and see whether yours is a reasonably good match.

With regard to *description*, dropping and breaking items was the primary behavior that occurred, occasionally accompanied by yelling. Some other behaviors (kicking, biting others) that had presumably been identified during an initial interview were not observed. This absence might indicate that more information

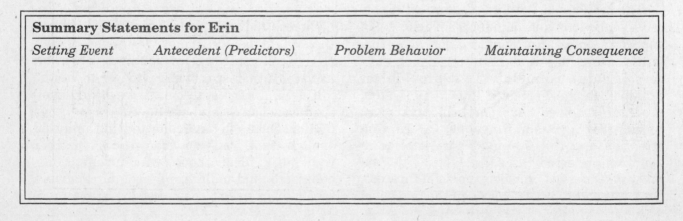

Summary Statements for Erin

Setting Event	*Antecedent (Predictors)*	*Problem Behavior*	*Maintaining Consequence*

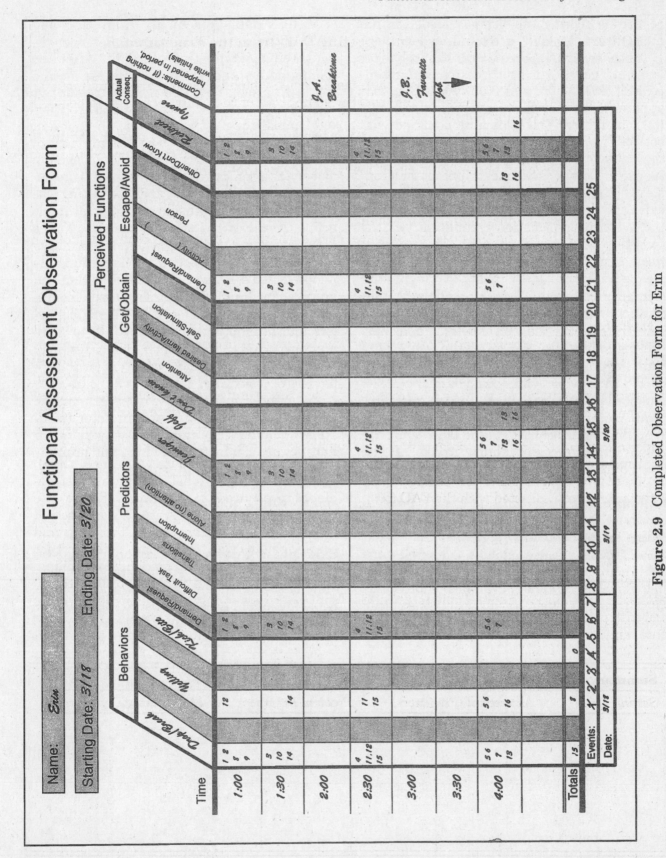

Figure 2.9 Completed Observation Form for Erin

regarding kicking and biting is needed or that more direct observation should be done.

With regard to *predictors,* the behaviors were not coded during three particular time periods (2:00, 3:00, and 3:30) when Erin was apparently on a break or involved in preferred work activities. The behaviors occurred with both of Erin's primary support persons. Most of the behaviors were coded as occurring in response to Demands/Requests, except for a couple of occasions when the observer was unsure what the predictor event might have been.

Given this information about predictors, the recorders understandably felt the behaviors were serving the *function* of allowing Erin to escape from demands/requests. While the staff primarily redirected Erin to work activities, this action may have allowed her at least temporarily to escape the task or activity demands.

This information would lead to a variety of potential programming strategies. Erin's schedule of tasks and activities could be changed, she could be taught or prompted to use more appropriate communicative responses instead of dropping and breaking, and she could be given more frequent short breaks. These types of issues are discussed in Chapter 4.

Example 2: Peter Data on Peter's problem behaviors during part of the day in his home setting are presented in Figure 2.10. As you did with Erin, take a few minutes to study Peter's data, then write some summary statements in the space labeled "Summary Statements for Peter." Then (and only then!) you can compare your statements with those listed in Appendix F.

Peter's data present an interesting pattern. With regard to *description,* Peter consistently engaged in either biting his wrist and grabbing/pushing, or biting his wrist and hitting his face. Thus, there appear to be two classes of behaviors. Both occurred at different times during the day and in different situations or contexts. The consistent *predictor* for biting and grabbing was being engaged in shaving and self-care routines by staff. The consistent predictor for biting and face hitting was being in a situation with no attention or interaction. *Perceived functions* of the two classes of behavior were gaining attention (for biting and face hitting) and escaping the presumably nonpreferred self-care activities (for biting and grabbing/pushing). The primary actual consequence involved staff blocking Peter's behaviors and attempting to redirect him to more appropriate activities. Such responses may have provided reinforcing attention for the behaviors occasionally.

As with Erin, a number of programmatic strategies might be considered in Peter's situation, including changing the way self-care routines are conducted, teaching and prompting more appropriate alternative communicative behaviors to get attention and breaks, and providing "noncontingent" attention on a more frequent basis.

Example 3: Curtis This example brings us back to Curtis, whom we met in talking about functional assessment interviews (see Figure 2.2). Figure 2.11 presents observation data on Curtis in his school setting. Take a few min-

---

Summary Statements for Peter

Setting Event	Antecedent (Predictors)	Problem Behavior	Maintaining Consequence

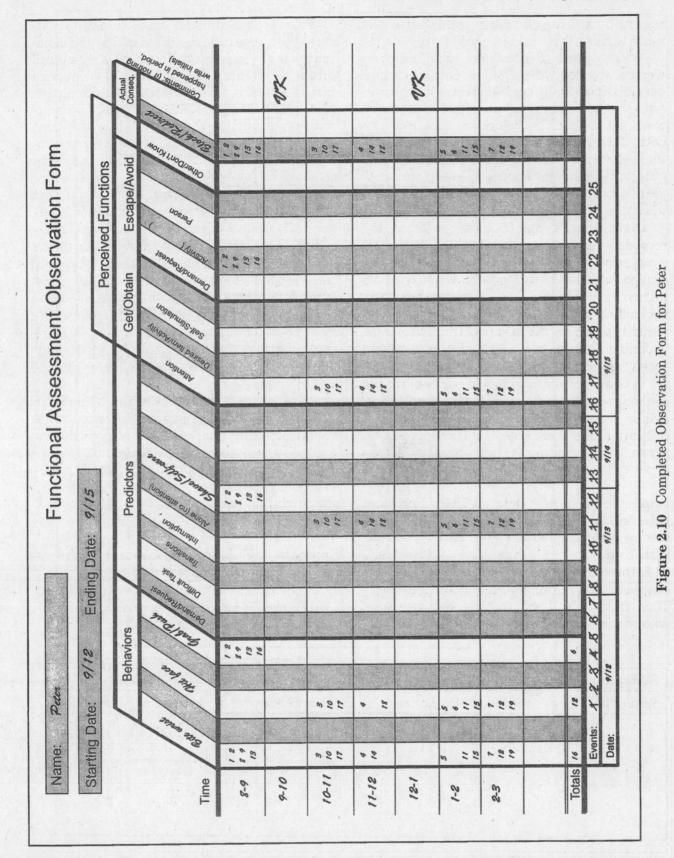

Figure 2.10 Completed Observation Form for Peter

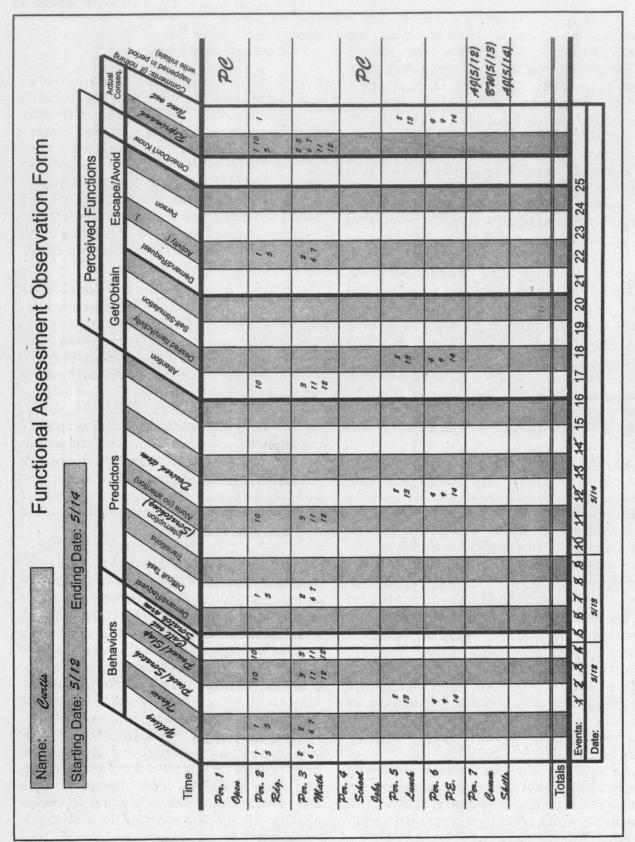

Figure 2.11 Completed Observation Form for Curtis

utes to study the data. Then go back to the summary statements presented in Section K of Figure 2.2, based on the completed interview with Curtis's teachers. Do you believe the observation data provide support for the initial summary statements, or should they be revised based on the data? (After you have done this, you can check your conclusions with the statements for Curtis presented in Appendix F.)

Curtis's data validate three primary patterns. During reading and math, he engages in either yelling and throwing, or pounding and slapping his desk and calling out. Yelling and throwing were preceded by being asked to do difficult tasks and were coded as serving the function of escaping from those activities. Pounding/slapping and calling out were preceded by situations in which Curtis was receiving little direct attention; they were coded as serving the function of obtaining such attention. The periodic reprimands may be inadvertently reinforcing and helping to maintain the attention-motivated behaviors.

In the third pattern, Curtis is engaged in aggressive behaviors (pinching/scratching) to get desired items from peers. This action typically resulted in a time-out, a strategy that appeared not to have a substantial effect on eliminating the aggression, as Curtis continued to use these behaviors across the 3 days of observation. During the 3 days of observation, the arm-scratching behavior described in the interview did not occur. Therefore, disruptive behavior following an interruption in the scratching also was not observed. It would be important to follow up on such a finding to decide whether it was only a temporary or idiosyncratic occurrence or whether perhaps a medical or other type of intervention had resolved the problem for the time being.

As with the other examples, a number of programming strategies might be considered in this situation. Curtis's case is discussed in Chapter 3, which addresses program development and implementation.

Decision Making Based on Observational Data

Once a sufficient amount of data are available, several decisions can be made including (1) gathering additional data to learn whether patterns and relationships become clearer; (2) conducting systematic functional analysis manipulations to clarify or confirm particular behavior patterns (see later sections); or (3) beginning program development and implementation based on the interview and observation data collected. Providing strict rules about such decision making is difficult.

Gathering further observational data

We have recommended that observers initially gather data for 2–5 days or until they have a minimum of 15–20 occurrences of behaviors to examine. This is a reasonable point at which to look at the data and assess whether the patterns observed are consistent with the initial summary statements based on the interview information. If consistent patterns of behaviors, predictors, and apparent functions are evident and these are consistent with your summary statements, you have probably collected enough data and are ready to move to program development and implementation.

However, if the patterns are *not* clear, then gathering data for another 2–5 days may be helpful to see whether consistent relationships begin to emerge. At this point you might also want to do two things. First, review and, if necessary, troubleshoot your data collection process to make sure that all observers have a clear and consistent idea of what they are doing and how they should be doing it. At the same time, you also may want to review the summary statements developed from your interview information. Consider whether these statements continue to be adequate or appropriate guides for your direct observation process. After additional direct observation data are collected, you can look again to decide whether things are starting to sort themselves out.

If they have not, the persons involved should *consider* moving to another step, which is to conduct systematic functional analysis manipulations to try to pinpoint and/or eliminate some variables that may be influencing the problem behaviors. These functional analyses should be focused on the variables and events that appear to most likely be related to the problem behaviors, based on the assessment information gathered to that point. The next section defines and presents examples of such manipulations and offers procedures and guidelines for carrying them out.

Functional Analysis Manipulations

For most functional assessments, the use of interviews and direct observations will lead to summary statements that identify clear patterns regarding predictors of problem behaviors and the consequences that maintain them, or their functions. However, if the information obtained from the assessment interviews and direct observations fails to reveal consistent patterns of behavior or if summary statements cannot be clearly confirmed through direct observation data, the next strategy to consider is conducting systematic functional analysis manipulations. Functional analysis is designed specifically to test hypotheses regarding variables or events most strongly related to the occurrence of problem behaviors. Consider, for example, that your summary statement (hypothesis) indicated that Eileen was most likely to scream and hit others when she was given tasks that were hard, and you believe her problem behavior is maintained by escaping these hard tasks. You may test elements of this summary statement by first giving Eileen easy tasks for 10 minutes, taking a break, then giving her hard tasks for 10 minutes, then easy tasks, then hard tasks. If she does good work when given a task, she receives the usual praise. If she begins even the smallest problem behavior, the work is removed for a minute and she is instructed to "cool down." If problem behaviors are much more likely to

be observed during hard tasks than during easy tasks, and if removing the work results in a temporary rapid reduction in the problem behaviors, then the functional analysis would have validated your hypothesis.

If your summary statement for Eileen had indicated that when given seat work of any type she was likely to engage in screaming and hitting to gain attention, the functional analysis for Eileen might include conditions in which she (a) works on tasks alone and receives attention as soon as she begins problem behaviors, and (b) works on the same tasks with one-to-one support. If the results indicate that problem behaviors occurred only when she was not getting attention and were unrelated to type of task, this finding again would validate the hypotheses defined in your summary statement.

The basic focus of a functional analysis is to identify associations between events in the environment (antecedents and/or consequences) and problem behaviors. The process may involve comparing many different conditions to test the summary statement hypothesis, but the basic idea is to test whether situations in which you predict problem behaviors to occur actually are associated with problem behaviors, *and* whether situations in which you predict problem behaviors not to occur are associated with low levels of problem behavior. Functional analysis is the only approach that allows documentation of a true functional relationship and thus provides the greatest possible precision and confidence in building our understanding of when, where, and why problem behaviors occur.

Although functional analysis procedures may be used in typical school or community settings, they have been used most often in the context of research activities (see references in Appendix A). The precision and variety of methods reported in the literature are rapidly increasing and have provided a framework for conducting functional analyses in applied settings. However, several concerns and issues need to be considered before functional analysis procedures are carried out.

When Should Functional Analysis Be Done?

The benefit of the precision offered by functional analysis must be balanced against the time, technical skill, and extra attention to safety that this approach requires. A functional analysis demands high levels of skill if it is to be carried out effectively and may often require that informed consent and human subjects' approval be obtained. This is why we recommended earlier that a functional analysis be conducted only if the data collected using the FAI and FAO are unclear.

Who Should Be Involved?

A functional analysis typically is a team effort. *It is important, however, that someone with direct supervised experience in conducting functional analysis manipulations guide the process.* If this expertise is not available within the team or if the person responsible for the initial parts of the assessment process is not trained in functional analysis, the team leader needs to seek additional assistance from a person with these skills. The number of other people involved would depend primarily on potential safety issues. Because a functional analysis may involve the occurrence of serious problem behavior, you may need several persons available to maintain safety and adequate control over potentially difficult situations. For example, if there is a likelihood that the person may engage in self-injurious behaviors such as head banging or self-biting, then enough people are needed to provide protection (including appropriate medical personnel). If the person is likely to run from the functional analysis setting, ensuring sufficient staff to prevent the person from escaping would be necessary. *Functional analysis manipulations should not be carried out unless appropriate safeguards are available.* These issues are discussed in more detail in the section entitled "Important Considerations and Guidelines."

The Process of Conducting a Functional Analysis

An extensive body of research on functional analysis procedures has been produced by a number of applied researchers. A reference/resource list on functional analysis research is provided in Appendix A, and readers are referred to this list for detailed information on functional assessment and analysis procedures. This section of the handbook offers a general overview of the methods but insufficient depth for someone to learn and use the technology independently. Our goal is to provide a foundation and enough detail that the reader could be effective when working with a person trained in functional analysis methods.

Basic approaches The basic process of a functional analysis involves presenting different environmental events or situations and observing how they affect a person's behavior. Two different approaches have been described in the research literature and used in applied settings, both singly and in combination. One approach involves the manipulation of structural or antecedent events. These include presenting particular requests or instructions, asking the person to participate in certain activities, having a particular person present, conducting interactions in a particular setting, or leaving the person alone or without attention for a time. These activities are done to test ideas or hypotheses about which events or variables might predict the onset of behaviors.

The second approach focuses primarily on the manipulation of consequences for the problem behaviors. Different situations are arranged and specific consequences are provided contingent upon the occurrence of specific problem behaviors. For example, a child might be told to play alone while an adult tends to some work. If the child begins to scream or hit, the adult might provide brief contingent attention (such as "Please don't scream; it's time for you to play now") and then return to work. In another situation, an adult might be asked to do a particular task or activity and then be allowed to have a break or briefly escape from the task, contingent on the occurrence of problem behaviors. If higher rates of problem behaviors are seen when particular consequences are delivered, one can conclude that those consequences are likely to be maintaining the behaviors.

In some cases, elements of both types of approaches might be used during an assessment. For example, a child might be exposed to task demands of various types so that observers can see which ones are more likely to lead to problem behaviors. However, in each type of situation, escape would be provided in the form of a brief break, contingent on the occurrence of problem behaviors.

Deciding what to assess Based on the results of your interviews and observations, you should have at least one idea or hypothesis about the behaviors of concern, in the form of what we have called summary statements. Following are typical examples of such statements: (a) When there is little activity, Mary flicks her fingers to obtain visual stimulation; (b) When the teacher is attending to other students, Michael yells to get her attention; (c) When Jodece sees a favorite object, she screams and runs to grab it; (d) When Katie makes a mistake in class, she runs from the room to avoid negative attention in the form of teasing from peers; (e) When Ronald is involved in a task in which he makes several mistakes, he hits the teacher to escape from the difficult task.

To test these summary statements directly, we must observe the person under conditions in which particular relevant antecedents and consequences are present and under conditions in which they are not present. Put simply, we set up conditions (antecedents and/or consequences) in which we expect to see increases or high rates of problem behavior, and then observe problem behaviors to determine whether this expected effect actually happens. We also set up conditions in which we do not expect high rates of problem behaviors and observe these as a compari-

son. By doing these manipulations and observing problem behaviors changing across the conditions we present, we can determine which variables actually influence problem behaviors.

Different functional analysis design strategies Two basic types of single-case research designs have been used most frequently in conducting functional analyses. These are the reversal (ABAB) design and the multi-element (alternating treatments) design. A reversal design (ABAB) involves (a) gathering data during an initial or *baseline* (A) phase when the variable of interest is not present; (b) conducting a second *treatment or manipulation* (B) phase in which the event or situation of interest is present; and (c) repeating the alternation of these baseline and manipulation conditions to establish a clear pattern showing the relationship between the variable manipulation and changes in levels or rates of problem behaviors. For example, alternating blocks of teaching sessions that involve difficult tasks versus sessions that include only easy tasks would help identify a relationship between task difficulty and problem behaviors. If problem behaviors are consistently higher during difficult task phases, the hypothesis that the person performs problem behaviors to escape or end difficult task situations is supported.

A multi-element or alternating treatment design involves presenting several different conditions in an interspersed pattern within a relatively short period of time. Quite often the different conditions presented manipulate the consequences that are provided contingent on the occurrence of problem behaviors. Users of this method for functional analysis often use conditions, or variations on conditions, described by Iwata, Dorsey, Slifer, Bauman, and Richman (1982/1994). For example, sessions of difficult instruction in which escape is provided contingent on problem behaviors, sessions in which social attention is provided contingent on the problem behaviors, and sessions in which tangible objects (such as toys) are provided contingent on the problem behaviors may be interspersed with a "control" condition (such as sessions of nondemanding social play or interaction with the person) that is unlikely to result in problem behaviors. Sometimes a person may be left alone in some sessions—but is monitored appropriately for safety—so observers can determine whether problem behaviors occur when no external consequences are provided. The purpose of alternating and interspersing sessions of the different conditions over a period of time is to allow identification of the variables that have a substantial and consistent effect on problem behaviors. Typically, each condition is repeated at least a few times to allow observers to note whether any differences become apparent among conditions. If there are no clear initial differences, additional sessions may be run to help observers determine whether such differences will begin to be apparent.

Dealing with inconclusive analyses It is possible that clear patterns will not emerge for an individual, even with several repetitions of different conditions. In such a case, it is important for you to decide whether the conditions were correctly and consistently implemented. For example, were the difficult tasks *really* difficult for that person? Was the person affected by seeing or hearing people during a session in which he or she was supposed to be alone? You may need to modify conditions or situations and then present them again to get a clear picture of the antecedents and maintaining consequences of the behavior. Or you may need to identify other antecedent conditions or consequences that may actually be affecting the occurrence of problem behaviors. New hypotheses may need to be developed and then tested through functional analysis.

Ideas for Testing Different Types of Summary Statements

Obtaining internal stimulation Some behaviors may appear to serve a self-stimula-

tory function for a person; that is, they seem to provide some type of internal feedback that the person likes. Some authors refer to this type of relationship as one of "automatic reinforcement" because the performance of the behavior "automatically" results in the reinforcement. This type of summary statement is often difficult to confirm, but strategies exist for doing so. One strategy is to look at behavior in situations in which a person is alone, without materials or activities. This might mean leaving a person alone in a room while monitoring them unobtrusively through a window or open door. If the behaviors are more frequent under these conditions than others, they may serve such a self-stimulatory function. Another strategy is to try to prevent or block the stimulation that the behaviors provide and to see whether this tactic serves to decrease the behaviors. In one study, goggles were used to block the visual stimulation provided to the person by eye poking and rubbing. However, such blocking can be difficult or impossible for some behaviors, such as finger flapping and rocking, without becoming excessively intrusive. In these situations it is hard to sort out possible self-stimulatory effects from the effects of the interaction that is provided during the blocking.

Responding to aversive internal stimulation A variety of medical or physical conditions can result in pain or discomfort. A person's behaviors may be motivated by his or her attempts to escape or reduce these sensations. However, it would not only be difficult but also unethical to attempt to intentionally produce a headache, sinus infection, allergic reaction, or menstrual discomfort to observe their effect on a person. One way to attempt to assess such influences would involve providing a reasonable treatment for the condition when people suspect it is occurring and observing whether the behaviors decrease. For example, if a person engages in self-injurious head-hitting and rocking when he or she is also exhibiting a runny nose and watery eyes, administering an allergy relief medication and an analgesic (aspirin or ibuprofen) may result in reductions in the behaviors. *It is very important that this type of procedure be conducted in collaboration with a medical professional.* Parents, teachers, and program staff should not attempt to diagnose and treat potential medical problems on their own.

Obtaining social attention If you thought that the person was engaging in the behaviors to obtain social attention or interaction, you could set up conditions under which the behaviors were successful in recruiting attention and conditions under which they were not successful. For example, a child could be asked to work or play quietly in a room while an adult works in another area. In one situation, the adult would respond to the child when the behaviors occurred ("please do not do that"). In another situation, the staff person would ignore and not respond to those behaviors. If the behaviors were more frequent during the conditions that resulted in attention, this observation would support the hypothesis that the function of the behaviors is to gain attention. (Note that for such differences to become apparent may take some time or a number of sessions, especially if the behaviors have been intermittently or inconsistently reinforced in the past.)

Obtaining desired objects or activities Individuals may engage in problem behavior when they appear to want access to an object or activity. This hypothesis can be tested by setting up situations in which a desired object or activity is present but not initially accessible. If the person attempts to approach and grab the item, she or he would be prevented. The item would be given only contingent on the occurrence of problem behaviors ("OK, you can have the _____"). Typically, after a brief period, the item would be taken back, and a new opportunity or trial would begin. The person's behavior in these types of situations could be compared with his or her actions in other situations in which the items or activities are not present or are made freely available to the person independent of the occurrence of problem behaviors.

Avoidance of social attention, requests, or activities A person's behaviors may be motivated by escaping or avoiding social attention (in response to a greeting, such as "So, Mitch, tell me how you've been?"), task requests, or other nonpreferred activities or interactions. This hypothesis can be assessed by creating situations in which such attention, tasks, or activities are presented, and then a brief period of escape (perhaps 30 seconds) is provided contingent on the occurrence of problem behaviors. The person's responses under these conditions can be compared to his or her behavior in other sessions in which the demands or activities are not present (such as a nonsocial toy play condition).

Conducting manipulations during typical routines Conducting manipulations during a person's typical schedule of activities in his or her normal setting would be the most valid approach for carrying out a functional analysis. For example, we could schedule a desired manipulation, such as presenting a difficult task demand, several times during the person's regular instructional periods. This task presentation could periodically be presented and removed to see what would happen. The number of times the manipulations would have to be presented and removed would depend on the size of the effects and how quickly they were obtained. This type of approach would help to ensure that the situations and influential variables identified as problematic are most likely to be valid and relevant to what actually goes on with a person on a day-to-day basis.

Examples of Functional Analysis Manipulations

This section presents examples based on work we have conducted with persons performing problem behaviors. Figure 2.12 presents data from an example in which antecedent conditions were manipulated using a reversal (ABAB) design. Greg was a middle school student with severe disabilities; he would yell and engage in aggressive behavior (hitting

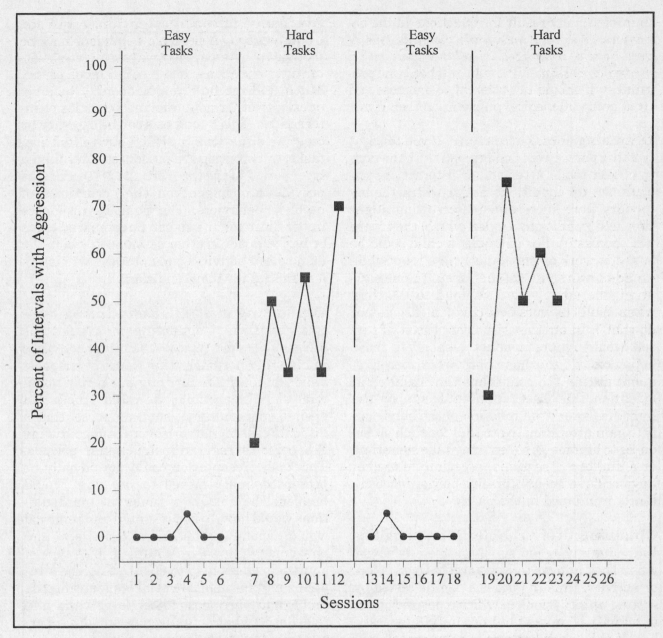

Figure 2.12 Functional Analysis Manipulation of Antecedent Conditions
(Easy Versus Hard Tasks) for Greg

and grabbing) during instruction. When he hit, his teacher took him to a time-out chair in the corner of the classroom. Based on an interview and observations, we summarized that Greg used aggressive behavior *primarily* to escape from difficult tasks that resulted in the teacher's providing some form of error correction ("Stop, please; you need to do it this way"). To learn whether this was the case, Greg's teacher conducted several teaching sessions that involved only tasks that were familiar and that he could easily complete. Following this, sessions involving less familiar tasks that were more difficult were conducted. These easy and hard task conditions were then repeated to confirm the effects. The graph in Figure 2.12 demonstrates that the frequency of Greg's aggressive behavior

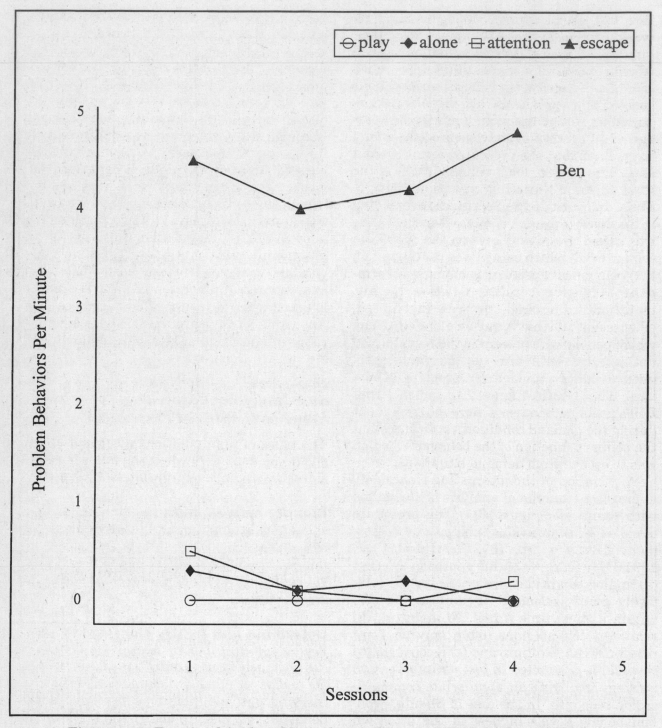

Figure 2.13 Functional Analysis Manipulation of Consequence Conditions for Ben

was consistently higher when harder tasks were presented. These data confirmed the initial summary statement that aggressive behavior was serving an escape function for Greg.

Figure 2.13 illustrates functional analysis manipulations carried out with Ben, an elementary student who attended class at his local school. Ben's problem behaviors of concern included hitting or slapping his head and face, and also mouthing or biting his hand. He would engage in these behaviors during instruction, during classroom activities, or even when a teacher or class assistant approached him. An interview and direct observations had led to a hypothesis that these behaviors served an escape function. Ben's teacher carried out a functional analysis procedure for 4 days. Each day she presented four different situations to Ben, for 5 minutes each, in the form of an alternating treatment design. These four included a play situation (listening to his favorite music), a demand situation (he was asked to activate keys on the classroom computer) in which escape was contingent on the occurrence of problem behaviors, a contingent attention condition (when he hit, mouthed, or rocked, he was instructed, "Please don't do that"), and an alone condition where people were present in the room but did not interact with him (no external consequences were provided for problem behaviors). The data in Figure 2.13 indicate that Ben's problem behaviors were most frequent during the demand condition, confirming that the primary function of the behaviors for Ben was to escape from demand situations.

A variation of the alternating treatments approach to functional analysis is illustrated with Shante (see Figure 2.14). This procedure is called brief functional analysis or assessment (Derby et al., 1992; Northup et al., 1991). Key features of this approach are that (a) analog conditions are presented for relatively brief sessions (10 minutes or less) within a short time frame (90 minutes), (b) relatively few sessions (often only one) are run for each condition, and (c) a contingency reversal is conducted to test an intervention strategy involving an appropriate communication response. In the case of Shante, problem behavior was highest in the attention condition, supporting a hypothesis that problem behaviors functioned to get attention. An appropriate communication response (saying "Come here, please") did not occur during the assessment phase. During the first contingency reversal phase session, the appropriate communication response of saying "Come

here, please" was first modeled for Shante, and then she was prompted to use the appropriate response, which was reinforced with attention. The problem behaviors did not produce attention during this session. Note that problem behaviors were very low and that use of the appropriate communication response was high when attention was delivered only for saying "Come here, please." A reversal back to attention for problem behaviors, followed by a second session of attention for "Come here, please," confirms that the attention function is primary and that teaching the appropriate communication response is an effective intervention strategy. There are many possible variations of the basic functional analysis procedures presented here. The reader is encouraged to review other resources (see Appendix A) to learn more about the full range of functional analysis procedures.

Important Considerations and Guidelines Concerning Functional Analysis Procedures

The types of manipulations discussed above should be done *only* when the following considerations can be appropriately addressed.

Identify specific features to assess You should not attempt manipulations unless the initial assessment activities have resulted in information or summary statements that provide guidance on specific situations and variables to assess.

Determine and justify the level of risk Severe self-injurious or aggressive behavior can obviously be very dangerous for individuals and/or teaching and support staff. Before carrying out manipulations involving such behaviors, we need to determine the level of potential risk and decide whether taking those risks is justified by the potential outcomes.

Control relevant variables Functional analysis manipulations should be done only when you can readily control relevant situ-

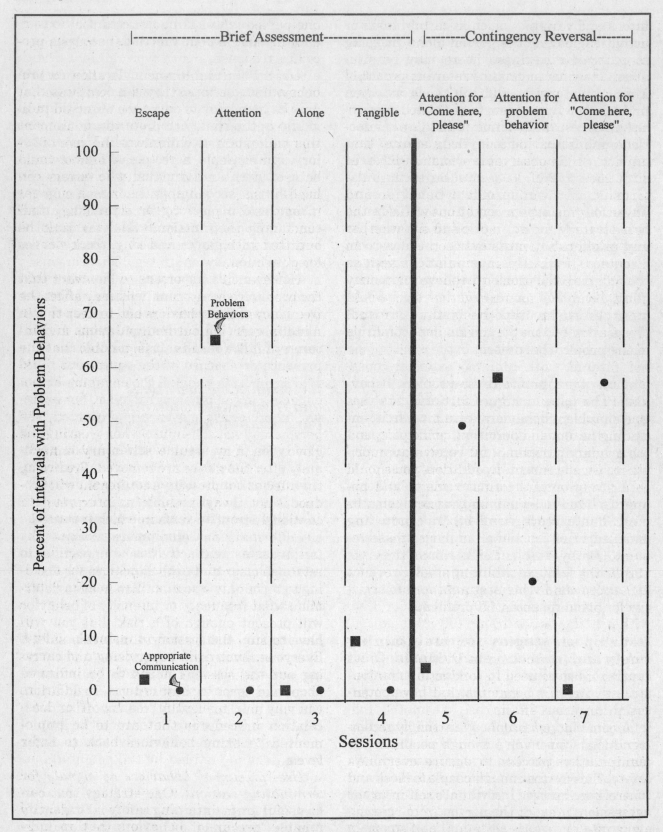

Figure 2.14 An Example of Brief Functional Assessment with Shante

ations and variables, such as certain tasks or activities, leaving the person alone, or going to particular settings. There may be situations in which controlling relevant aspects of a situation may be difficult, such as when problem behaviors seem to be related to *internal* physical events (sinus or middle ear infections, menstrual periods, drug effects) that are not readily observable or manipulable. In such cases, careful observation of the relationship between problem behavior and physical symptoms or conditions would be the best strategy for attempting to see whether any relationship exists between the two. As discussed previously, manipulations such as providing medications to relieve pain may affect behavior, an observation that would strengthen the hypothesis that internal physical events are playing an important role in the problem behavior.

Obtain appropriate reviews and approvals Prior to conducting functional analyses you should inform all relevant persons, including parents, supervisors, principals, and other administrators, and receive appropriate informed consent. In addition, you should obtain appropriate formal reviews and approvals from relevant supervisory committees. The factors involved in conducting manipulations are often similar to those required for an intervention plan and the risks may be the same, so obtaining similar reviews and approvals is the most appropriate strategy for avoiding potential problems.

Develop strategies for maintaining safety and protecting individuals Great caution must be used in conducting manipulations involving behaviors that have potentially dangerous effects.

Involve enough people. We strongly recommend that you involve enough people in the manipulation process to ensure everyone's safety. This means enough people to block and control the observed individual's self-injury or aggression, prevent the person from running away into an unsafe situation, and so on. In addition, the procedure must involve at least one person who has had substantial experience in carrying out functional analysis procedures.

Use protective equipment. To allow certain behaviors to occur so they can be assessed, it may be necessary to outfit the observed individual or the staff with protective equipment that minimizes or eliminates the risk of injury. For example, a protective helmet could be used with an individual who engages in head-hitting or banging. If a person engages in aggressive pinching or scratching, staff conducting the functional analysis could be outfitted with gloves and long, thick sleeves for protection.

However, it's important to be aware that the protective equipment itself may affect the frequency of the behaviors and to keep this in mind in carrying out manipulations and interpreting the results. It is possible that the presence or absence of the equipment could rapidly become a signal for engaging or not engaging in the problem behavior. For example, if protective gloves are presented, the person may not self-injure when wearing the gloves but may resume self-injury immediately after the gloves are removed. Predicting the effects that protective equipment will produce is not always possible, so interpret data cautiously from sessions in which it is used.

Set criteria for terminating sessions. Before sessions begin, it is *very* important to establish clear and explicit criteria for deciding to terminate a session. You need to determine what frequency or intensity of behavior will present enough of a risk that you will have to stop the session to maintain safety. Everyone involved in supervising and carrying out the sessions needs to be informed about and agree to these criteria. In addition, you may need to identify "cooling off" or deescalation procedures that are to be implemented to bring behaviors back to safer levels.

Use "precursor" behaviors as signals for terminating sessions. One strategy that can be useful for maintaining safety is to identify reliable "precursor" behaviors that an individual may exhibit prior to more intense and dangerous behaviors. Functional analysis sessions would then focus on the occurrence and nonoccurrence of these less intense and problematic behaviors. For example, if a person typically displays signs of agitation (e.g., rocking, pounding on a table) prior to self-injury or aggression, you can focus on the occurrence of those agitation behaviors during the assessment process. Once they occur, sessions could be terminated before the situation escalates to the occurrence of more dangerous behaviors.

Employ appropriate data collection and design procedures To obtain maximally useful information from functional analysis procedures, you must arrange to collect valid data on the behaviors of concern. This may require videotaping and later viewing and scoring the videotapes, or having designated individuals available to observe and collect data during sessions.

In addition, it is important that sessions be conducted in the context of appropriate design procedures. As we discussed, this means that variables should be presented and withdrawn in a reversal design approach or systematically presented across sessions in an alternating treatment format. Addressing these considerations will allow you to make the most reliable and valid conclusions about influential variables. A summary of guidelines for conducting functional analyses in applied settings is presented in Box 2.5.

Confirming and/or revising summary statements and moving to program development As with the direct observation strategies described above, one very important outcome of the functional analysis process should be either to validate or revise the summary statements that were developed based on initial assessment activities. Conducting a functional analysis should help you to support your summary statements or prompt you to revise them—toss one or more of them out or add new ones based on the data you have collected.

To this point, we have presented and discussed the major strategies for obtaining functional assessment information including interviews, direct observations, and manipulations. As we have stressed throughout this handbook, collecting such information is *not* an end in itself. The information is valuable only if it is used to guide the development and implementation of strategies for promoting adaptive behavior and reducing problem behavior. The next chapter focuses on the integration of functional assessment information to build support plans.

BOX 2.5 Guidelines for Conducting Functional Analysis Manipulations

1. Identify specific variables to be assessed during manipulations
2. Determine the level of risk that may be involved
3. Ensure that relevant variables can be controlled and manipulated
4. Obtain appropriate reviews and approvals
5. Have enough people available to maintain safety during sessions
6. Determine specific criteria for terminating sessions if needed
7. Consider the use of protective equipment for individuals and/or teaching/support staff
8. Consider using precursor behaviors as signals for terminating sessions
9. Employ appropriate data collection and design procedures

Building Behavior Support Plans

The purpose of functional assessment is to increase the effectiveness and efficiency of behavior support plans. You should always strive to make sure there is a logical connection between the gathering of assessment information and the development of behavior support plans. This section of the handbook provides a process for using functional assessment results to design plans of support. Chapter 3 presents broad considerations that should guide the development and implementation of a plan as well as a process for selecting intervention procedures. Chapter 4 suggests specific formats for writing, implementing, and evaluating behavior support interventions.

Four Considerations for Building Behavior Support Plans

Four broad themes are important in the design of behavioral support plans: (a) the plan should indicate how staff, family, or support personnel will change and not just focus on how the person of concern will change; (b) the plan should be directly based on the func-

tional assessment information; (c) the plan should be technically sound—that is, consistent with the principles and laws of human behavior; and (d) the plan should be a good fit with the values, resources, and skills of the people responsible for implementation.

Behavior Support Plans *Describe* Our *Behavior*

Behavior support plans are designed to alter patterns of problem behavior. The process by which this is done, however, involves change in the behavior of family, teachers, staff, or managers in various settings. Plans of behavior support define what *we* will do differently. It is the change in our behavior that will result in improved behavior of the focus person. The plan may involve changes we will make in the physical setting, changes in curriculum, changes in the medications we will administer, changes in schedule, changes in how we teach, and changes in rewards and punishers. A good behavior support plan defines in very specific detail the changes expected in the behavior of relevant teachers, family members, or staff. It is change in our behavior that will result in change in the behavior of people with disabilities.

Behavior Support Plans Should Build from Functional Assessment Results

Functional assessment information should allow us to identify specific changes in a classroom, home, or workplace that will change patterns of problem behaviors. Too often functional assessments are completed but have no impact on the procedures used in the plan of behavioral support. If behavior analysis is the design of environments that promote appropriate behavior, then functional assessment is a tool for identifying key features of an effective environment.

Two strategies have proven useful to improve the link between functional assessment outcomes and behavior support plan design. The first is simply to ensure that the summary statements from the functional assessment are listed in the behavior support plan. These statements provide the foundation for the plan, and *all* procedures defined in the behavior support plan should be logically consistent with the statements. If, for example, the summary statement indicated that problem behaviors were maintained by access to attention, the intervention should not involve contingent delivery of attention (even "negative" attention) following the problem behavior. If the summary statement indicated that problem behaviors were maintained by escape from tasks, then separating the person from the task contingent upon problem behaviors (for example, time-out) should be avoided.

A second strategy has been to build a "model" of the functional assessment summary statement and define how the model must be changed to ensure that appropriate behaviors will "compete" successfully with problem behaviors. Behavior plans must indicate not only what a person should *not* do; they should also indicate what the individual *should* do. We should not assume that if a functional assessment is conducted an obvious intervention plan will emerge. The critical process of working through the functional assessment results to build a plan is one of the major challenges in the field of applied behavior analysis.

Behavior Support Plans Should Be Technically Sound

Human behavior follows certain empirical principles, and any clinical plan of behavioral support should be consistent with those principles. Behavior management is not just a set of techniques (time-out, response cost, overcorrection, token economies) but includes a set of foundation principles that can be applied in a wide array of formats. Reinforcement, punishment, generalization, and stimulus control are examples of such principles that should serve as the technical foundation of any plan of behavioral support. Such a plan should use these kinds of principles to build from the functional assessment summary toward an environment that logically supports adaptive behavior and reduces the occurrence of problem behavior.

Designing technically sound plans of support is not easy. To complicate matters, many people responsible for behavioral support have not had substantial training in integrating and applying complex behavioral principles. In most cases, however, plans of behavioral support will be technically sound if they make the problem behaviors *irrelevant, inefficient,* and *ineffective.*

Make problem behaviors *irrelevant* Developers of the plan should identify those situations (stimulus conditions) that set the occasion for problem behaviors and organize the environment to reduce the likelihood that these conditions are encountered. For example, if Jason finds seat work very aversive because of his inability to do the problems, changes in the complexity of the tasks or the amount of work he is asked to do can make escape-motivated problem behaviors irrelevant—that is, the features of the work that are aversive are no longer present. Similarly, if Eileen engages in screaming and stripping as ways of getting attention in an otherwise boring environment, her problem behaviors could become irrelevant if a more active and interesting schedule of daily events was developed for her. Making the problem behavior irrelevant typically involves structural changes: altering the physical settings, enriching the environment, improving the activities or curriculum, increasing predictability and choice options available to the person. These efforts alone may not eliminate the problem behavior, but they will make other elements of the support plan more effective.

Make problem behaviors *inefficient* The efficiency of a behavior refers to the combined effects of (a) the physical effort required for a person to perform the behavior, (b) the number of times the person must perform the behavior before he or she is reinforced (the schedule of reinforcement), and (c) the time delay between the first problem behavior and reinforcement. A child in a classroom who makes odd noises that are reinforced by peer attention typically performs a very efficient behavior: the reinforcer is obtained quickly after only *one* easy-to-do problem response. A young adult who engages in an extensive and severe tantrum to avoid demands may be engaging in an effective (the reward is obtained) but inefficient behavior (the tantrum is very effortful, many responses are required, and access to the reward may take a long time). The functional assessment should identify what is maintaining the problem behavior (such as attention, escape from tasks, access to preferred items) and provide some indication of the efficiency of the problem behavior (effort, schedule, time delay). Recall that the Functional Assessment Interview includes questions focusing on efficiency issues. When feasible, the support plan should define an alternative, socially appropriate, and *more efficient* way for the person to achieve the same reward. This concept is the foundation of an intervention approach known as functional communication training (or functional equivalence training) and has long been a general principle of good behavioral support.

A simple example of functional communication training was provided by a young boy, Kioshi, who did not speak and used intense aggression to obtain preferred toys and food. His aggression resulted in his getting what he wanted about 50% of the time, but it also required a lot of effort. When he was taught to use signs to make requests, the frequency of his aggression dropped to near zero. The signed requests were less effortful than grabbing and hitting, they were more likely to result in success (80% versus 50% of the time), and signing worked more quickly. The net effect was that the use of signs was both more socially acceptable and more efficient than aggression.

Make problem behaviors *ineffective* We have found that a person with a long history of problem behaviors will continue to perform them as long as those behaviors are effective (even when the individual has been taught alternatives to those problem behaviors). To the extent possible, behavior support plans should make problem behaviors ineffective ways of obtaining reinforcers. Even when the behavior support plan includes the teaching of new, more efficient alternative skills, efforts should be made to extinguish the problem behavior.

Extinction involves systematically withholding or preventing access to a reinforcing outcome that previously was delivered. If the reinforcer was access to toys or adult attention, the plan of support would indicate how these reinforcers would be withheld after problem behaviors. If the problem behavior was reinforced by escape from demands or difficult tasks, then extinction would involve making sure the problem behaviors were *not* followed by escape from these demands or tasks. In many cases, using extinction procedures is easier said than done. It may be possible in some cases simply to withhold consequences such as attention or affection. In other cases, the person may perform dangerous problem behaviors that simply cannot be ignored. With some individuals, it may be possible to withhold the reinforcer temporarily and redirect the person to the new, alternative communication response. For example, Todd's screaming and head hits may be maintained by escape from demanding tasks. You cannot ignore his self-injury.

When he begins the problem behaviors, however, you may temporarily withhold escape and instruct him to ask for a break the "right way" (verbally or with signs). Asking for a break also allows him to escape the task but in a socially appropriate, alternative form. This approach, however, creates the possible problem that Todd will learn a *chain* of behaviors. That is, he may learn to first scream, then hit his head, and then sign for a break. This problem can typically be avoided by teaching the person sign use initially in calmer contexts when the problem behaviors are not occurring and/or building in a brief delay between the appearance of the problem behavior and prompting the appropriate response.

The essential message is that plans of behavior support should be consistent with basic principles of behavior. In general, this consistency can be achieved if the elements of the plan have the effect of making problem behaviors *irrelevant, inefficient*, and *ineffective*.

Behavior Support Plans Should Fit the Setting Where They Will Be Implemented

Behavioral support procedures should be both technically sound *and* a good fit with the values, resources, and skills of the people who will implement the procedures. A number of different behavior support plans can always be used with a particular person in a particular context. The goal is not to build the one "perfect" plan but to design a plan that will be both effective and possible to implement. We can design a behavior plan that is technically brilliant only to find that staff are unwilling or unable to implement the procedures. The result is a plan that has minimal impact on the behavior of the staff and no impact on the behavior of the person being supported. If the plan is very expensive, effortful, or punishing to implement, we should not be surprised if the implementors do not adhere to its requirements faithfully.

Rian's behavior plan is a good example of this message. Rian was 7 years old and had severe intellectual disabilities. He escaped tasks that were difficult for him by kicking the people who made the task demands. This was most common during instructional sessions when he was being taught to use signs. He used signs in many situations but found sign use a difficult process and continued to deliver hard, accurate kicks to the legs of his teacher during sign training sessions. The initial plan conveyed to the teacher indicated that the curriculum was appropriate, that she needed to praise Rian for working on signs, and she needed to ignore his kicking. The teacher tried to follow this advice for a couple of sessions, developed an impressive pattern of bruises, and then began to discover many schedule conflicts that prevented her from offering future sign training sessions. The behavior plan might have been effective if it had been implemented, but the cost of implementation was too high for the teacher. A modified plan that focused on preventing Rian from kicking proved more workable as well as more successful for Rian.

If we expect plans of behavior support to change the behavior of families and staff, the procedures need to (a) fit the natural routines of the setting; (b) be consistent with the "values" of the people in the setting (they need to indicate a willingness to perform the procedures); (c) be efficient in terms of time, money, and resources; (d) be matched to the skills of the people who will carry out the procedures; and (e) produce reinforcing (not punishing) short-term results.

In summary, there are four important themes in developing behavior support plans: (a) clearly defining the needed changes in the behavior of the people implementing the plan; (b) emphasizing the logical link between the functional assessment results and the procedures employed; (c) being consistent with the basic principles of behavior; and (d) making a good fit with the values, skills, resources, and routines of the people who are expected to implement the plan.

Selecting Intervention Procedures: The Competing Behavior Model

Return now to the problem of linking the behavior support plan to the functional assessment results. It is common for clinicians to conduct a functional assessment and move directly into the writeup of the behavior support plan. We recommend that an intervening step be added once the functional assessment is completed. This step involves active collaboration with those people who will be implementing the plan and use of a *competing behavior model* to define the features of an effective environment. These features are then used to select the specific strategies that will make up the behavior support plan. We find the competing behavior model useful for the following reasons: (a) it increases the link between intervention procedures and functional assessment results; (b) it increases the fit between the values, skills, resources, and routines of the people who will carry out the plan and the procedures that will be employed; (c) it increases the logical coherence among the different procedures that could be used in a multi-element plan of support; and (d) it increases the fidelity with which the plan is ultimately implemented.

Constructing a Competing Behavior Model

Constructing a competing behavior model involves three steps. First, build a diagram of the functional assessment summary statements. Second, add appropriate behaviors that should compete with or replace the problem behaviors. And third, define intervention options that will promote appropriate behaviors and make problem behaviors irrelevant, inefficient, and ineffective. These steps are summarized in Box 3.1 and described below.

BOX 3.1 The Three Steps Involved in Completing a Competing Behavior Model

1. Diagram the functional assessment summary statements.
2. Define alternative or competing behaviors, and the contingencies associated with them.
3. Select intervention procedures that will make the problem behavior irrelevant, inefficient, and ineffective.

Step 1: Diagram functional assessment summary statements To diagram a functional assessment summary statement, simply list from left to right the (a) setting events; (b) antecedents (immediate predictors); (c) problem behaviors; and (d) maintaining consequences you identified in the summary statement. As an example, we found through a functional assessment that Derrick engaged in vomiting when presented with difficult "table" tasks (such as identifying letters and num bers). The vomiting was maintained by escaping from such tasks, and the vomiting was twice as likely to occur when he had slept fewer than 4 hours the night before. Therefore, the summary statement for Derrick was this: "When Derrick has had little sleep and is presented with difficult table tasks, he will engage in vomiting, which is maintained by escape from the tasks." The order of events in this functional assessment summary statement is shown in the following chart.

Setting Event	Antecedent (Predictors)	Problem Behavior	Maintaining Consequence
Fewer than 4 hours of sleep	Presentation of difficult table tasks	Vomit	Escape task

Below the chart, the statement is presented with arrows. Note that these arrows serve to emphasize the role of time in the sequence.

Fewer than 4 hours of sleep ⟶ Presentation of difficult table tasks ⟶ Vomit ⟶ Escape tasks

Consider another example in which Marlene, a 12-year-old student without disabilities, engages in frequent talking out during lectures in her seventh-grade biology class. The functional assessment indicates that her talking out is maintained by peer attention and occurs with increased likelihood when she has experienced negative social interactions with her peers earlier in the day. The summary statement would be this: "When Marlene has experienced negative peer social interactions during lectures, she will talk out to try to gain peer attention." The diagram for this statement follows.

Negative interactions ⟶ Biology lecture ⟶ Talking out ⟶ Peer attention

Yet another example is provided by 23-year-old Phillip, who has severe intellectual disabilities and spends long hours sitting in the corner of his bedroom rocking back and forth, flipping his right thumb against his upper lip. The functional assessment identified no "distant" setting events that affected his rocking and flipping and there did not appear to be any consistent events that predicted rocking and flipping. At first, staff suggested that Phillip engaged in rocking and finger flipping to gain the physical sensations these behaviors generated. However, after using the Functional Assessment Observation Form, they identified two patterns. One was that the rocking and flipping were more likely to occur when Phillip had no structured activi-ties; the other was that Phillip used rocking and flipping as an "anxi-ety" response. The two staff members who identified the second responsebegan to sit with Phillip and comfort him when they found him rocking. This led the staff to define three possible functions that were maintaining Phillip's rocking and flipping: (a) seeking physical sensation, (b) avoiding boredom, and (c) obtaining staff attention. When multiple functions are defined for a single situation, we have found it most helpful to select the *most powerful function* for attention. In this case, the staff identified "obtaining staff attention" as the most powerful of the presumed reinforcers. The summary statement for Phillip became: "When there are no structured activities, Phillip's rocking and flipping are maintained by access to staff attention." The summary statement diagram follows.

None identified ⟶ No ongoing activities ⟶ Rocking and finger flipping ⟶ Access to staff attention

Now, consider a person you have worked with and for whom you believe you can identify the more distant setting events, immediate predictors, problem behaviors, and maintaining consequences. Develop a summary statement that pulls together this information, and write it in the space below.

_____

_____

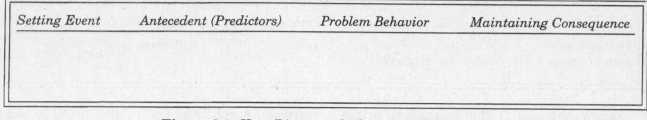

Setting Event	Antecedent (Predictors)	Problem Behavior	Maintaining Consequence

Figure 3.1 Your Diagram of a Summary Statement

In the space provided in Figure 3.1, diagram the summary statement. Include arrows to indicate the temporal sequences of events.

Step 2: Define alternative behaviors and the contingencies associated with those behaviors *A fundamental rule of effective behavioral support is that you should not propose to reduce a problem behavior without also identifying the alternative, desired behaviors the person should perform instead of the problem behavior.* Your plan of support will simultaneously target reduction of the problem behavior and an increase in desired behaviors. With this dual focus, it is helpful to identify clearly the behaviors or behavior paths that will be in competition with the problem behavior. We do this by asking two questions: (a) "Given that the setting and antecedent (predictor) events have occurred, what is the appropriate behavior you would like the person to perform in that situation?" and (b) "Given that the setting and antecedent (predictor) events have occurred, what would be a so-cially appropriate, 'equivalent' behavior that could produce the *same* consequence as the problem behavior?" The responses to these questions are added to the competing behavior model shown in Figure 3.2.

Think back to Derrick, who vomited when presented with difficult table tasks. The desired behavior for Derrick would be to do his task. But when his teacher was asked what happened when he completed his task, she said that he usually received some verbal praise and *more tasks* to do. When asked what equivalent behavior might be appropriate, the teacher's initial response was that there were no equivalent responses that were acceptable. After further discussion, she agreed that Derrick's asking for a break would be an acceptable response that would also produce the outcome of allowing him to escape the task, if only for a few minutes. Adding the desired behavior (perform task), equivalent behavior (ask for break), and their respective consequences to the competing behavior dia-

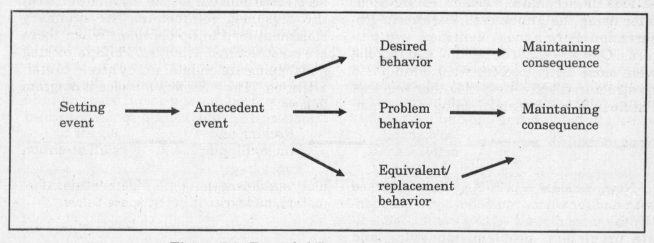

Figure 3.2 Expanded Competing Behavior Model

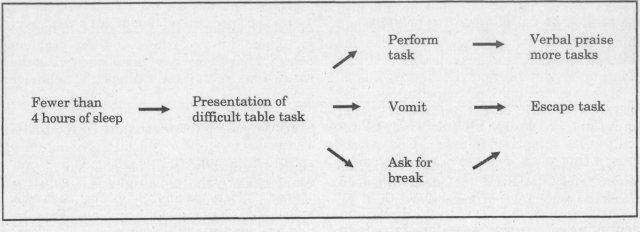

Figure 3.3 Derrick's Expanded Competing Behavior Model

gram for Derrick resulted in the diagram shown in Figure 3.3.

The competing behavior model for Derrick now shows (a) the functional assessment summary; (b) that there are minimal positive consequences for the desired behavior (performing tasks); and (c) that Derrick has no equivalent skills—such as asking for a break—that might allow him to escape from the task. The model also suggests that the difficult table tasks are aversive to him. When Derrick is presented with such tasks, they evoke escape-motivated behaviors. The tasks are even more likely to have this effect if Derrick is tired—has had fewer than 4 hours of sleep the previous night. This statement provides a great deal of information, and it is exactly the right type of information needed for designing an effective environment for Derrick.

Another example of building a competing behavior model was provided by Mara. Mara was 8 years old and had a very difficult home life. She did not have any disability labels but was continually getting into conflicts with her second-grade teacher for talking out, whining, refusing to work, noncompliance, and tantrums. The functional assessment for Mara indicated that her problem behaviors were very unlikely when she was working directly with the teacher, or in small groups with other children. Her problem behaviors appeared to function as a class (that is, they were maintained by the same consequence), were most likely to occur about 2 to 3 minutes after she was given a classroom assignment to complete independently, and were maintained by direct attention from the teacher (either positive or negative attention). A lack of consistent communication with Mara's family made it difficult to identify more distant setting events. The diagram of Mara's assessment information is shown in Figure 3.4.

Completing the competing behavior model involved first determining the desired behaviors. In this case the staff expected Mara to continue whatever activity was in progress. The consequence for continuing the activity was most likely to be more activity and little attention. The equivalent response identified

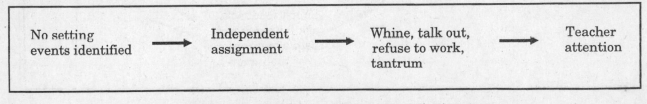

Figure 3.4 Mara's Assessment Information

was to ask verbally for teacher attention in the form of feedback or help. This was something Mara could do, but she did not use this skill effectively. The full competing behavior diagram for Mara appears in Figure 3.5.

When you are building competing behavior models, there will be many instances when equivalent and desired behaviors may be difficult or inappropriate to define. Our experience is that even in these cases, the model helps in the development of effective plans of support. Marlene's seventh-grade biology teacher, for example, was uninterested in identifying alternative ways for Marlene to obtain peer attention during his biology lectures. The competing behavior model for Marlene's talking out resulted in the diagram shown in Figure 3.6.

Now, return to the functional assessment diagram you developed (Figure 3.1) for the person and situation you know well. Duplicate that diagram in the top part of the form in Figure 3.7 (a blank copy is provided in Appendix G). Determine the "desired" behavior and place it above the problem behavior in your diagram. Consider what consequence typically occurs when the person performs this desired behavior; list that as the maintaining consequence. Once this is completed, define an equivalent behavior that is socially appropriate, is followed by the *same* conse-

quence as the problem behavior, and is easier and more efficient than the problem behavior. Place this behavior below the problem behavior. You have now completed two of the three steps in building a competing behavior model.

Step 3: Select intervention procedures
The goal is not to specify a single technique—such as time-out—that is expected to eliminate the problem behavior but to organize a cluster of changes in the setting that will reduce the likelihood of the problem behavior, that will increase the likelihood of the alternative appropriate behavior paths, and that fits the values, resources, and skills of the people who must implement the procedures. Your aim is to make the problem behavior irrelevant, inefficient, and ineffective.

A common approach in building behavior support plans is to begin with the consequences for the problem behavior. We have found, however, that starting with the consequences can sometimes lead to an excessive focus on this part of the plan, including the use of more intrusive procedures. Here is the process we recommend.

1. *Bring together those people who will have the task of implementing the behavior support plan.*

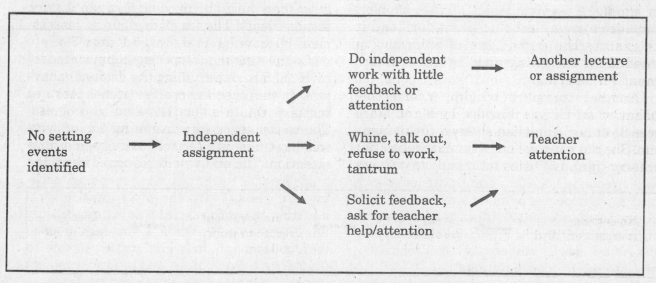

Figure 3.5 Competing Behavior Diagram for Mara

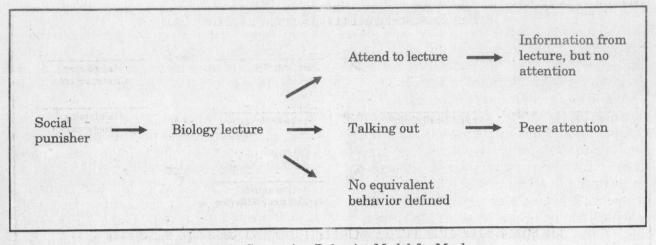

Figure 3.6 Competing Behavior Model for Marlene

2. *Diagram the competing behavior model, and review the logic and structure of the model.* There should be basic agreement on the functional assessment summary statements.

3. *Begin with more distant setting events and identify any changes that could make these events less likely or less influential.* Changes in setting events can make problem behaviors *irrelevant.* List your ideas for possible changes in the column in the setting event section of your competing behavior model in Figure 3.7.

4. *Focus next on changes in immediate antecedent events.* What changes can be made in immediate antecedents to make problem behaviors irrelevant? Consider the following: the daily schedule, the level of prompting or assistance, the curriculum or features of a task, the groupings in which work is done; you might provide more specific information about when tasks are to be done and when they will be completed, shorten task length, make tasks more relevant for the individual, intersperse easy tasks with hard tasks, provide precorrections for appropriate behaviors, and make expected behaviors more clear. List potential antecedent changes in the Predictor Strategies column in Figure 3.7. (See Appendix A for a more complete listing of references on antecedent manipulations.)

5. *List strategies for teaching and promoting desired and alternative behaviors.* Does the person need to be taught the desired or equivalent behaviors? Remember that knowing *how* to perform a skill is not sufficient. For a skill to be functional, the person must also know *when* to perform the skill. We often assume that because individuals have demonstrated that they are capable of a certain behavior they will use that behavior in all the appropriate situations. We may assume that they do not use the desired behavior in certain situations because they choose not to rather than because they have never been taught that the behavior is functional in that situation. The goal is to identify new behaviors we can teach the person that will be more efficient than the problem behaviors. Instruction should then focus on both *how* to perform those behaviors and how to discriminate *when* the new behaviors are appropriate.

Remember that teaching is among the most powerful behavior management tools at our disposal. In a very large number of situations, the key to effective reduction of problem behaviors is effective instruction of new behaviors. Learn how to teach. Learn the guidelines for selecting and sequencing teaching situations. Learn the procedures for presenting teaching trials so they convey unambiguous information. Learn how to teach both groups and individuals. Learn how to praise correct responses and ignore or correct errors. Learn how to use error patterns to adjust your instruction. Learn how to teach.

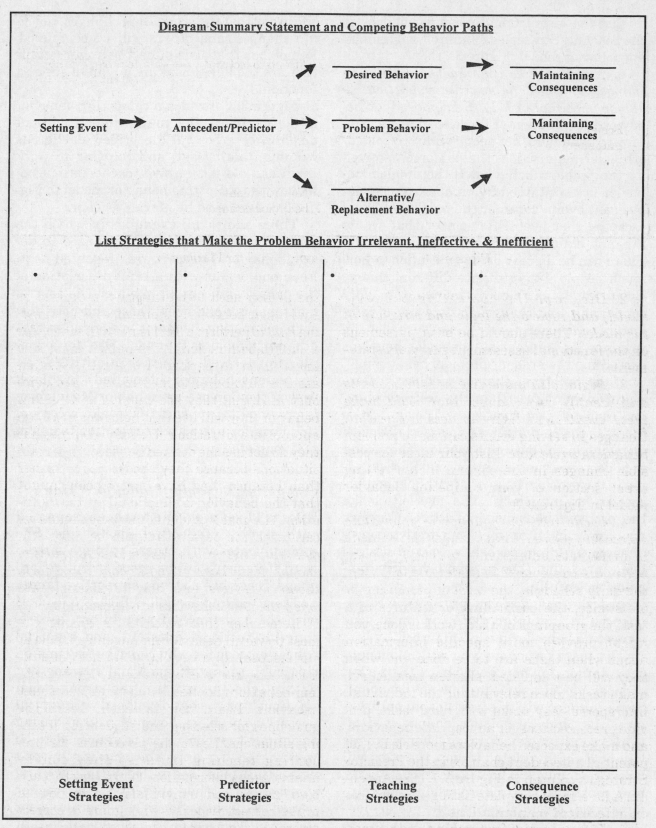

Figure 3.7 Competing Behavior Model Form

List the instructional recommendations in the Teaching Strategies column of your competing behavior model (Figure 3.7).

6. *Examine how consequences should be changed to make the positive, competing behavior path more likely.* Remember that behavior is a function of its consequences. You reward behaviors, not people. Start by considering the magnitude of the reinforcer received for the problem behavior. If the problem behavior is maintained by escape from an unpleasant event, consider the possible value of escaping that event. Remember that events are not equally reinforcing or punishing. There can be a great deal of variation in how much people like or dislike different things. Events can be extremely reinforcing or mildly reinforcing, and changes in the value of reinforcers occur continually. Make sure that the rewards for appropriate behavior equal or exceed the rewards for problem behaviors.

If the problem behavior produces a more powerful reinforcer than the desired behavior, consider two strategies. The first is to increase the reinforcer value associated with engaging in the desired behavior. The second is to decrease the reinforcer value for engaging in the problem behavior (withhold reinforcers or add punishers). The goal is to make the problem behavior ineffective. Consider how you can alter the comparative consequences for problem behaviors and desired behaviors to help the desired behaviors compete successfully.

List the changes you propose for consequences in the appropriate column of your competing behavior model (Figure 3.7).

The team of people who will implement the intervention now have before them a list of possible changes in the environment. Some changes will be structural in nature—alter the physical setting, change medications, modify schedules. Other changes will be directly related to how the staff will behave—changes in how tasks are presented, how reprimands are delivered, what reinforcers are used. Now have the group identify which of these ideas they believe are "doable." Determine with the group the spe-cific ways that the scheduling changes, teaching changes, and others will be completed. Remember that it is often the small details that are the key to making a plan of support functional.

Figure 3.8 provides a competing behavior model for Mara, the young woman without disabilities who was described earlier as whining, talking out, and refusing to work when she did not receive teacher attention. Review the competing behavior model in Figure 3.8, developed by Mara's teacher.

Three additional examples in which the competing behavior model was used to design behavioral support are presented next. Each one begins with a brief description of the person and context in which the assessment was done. Review these and note how each competing behavior model addresses different problems that can arise (for example, no desired behavior identified, no equivalent behavior identified). A blank copy of the Competing Behavior Model form is provided in Appendix G. Make a copy of this form for use with intervention teams in real contexts.

Competing Behavior Model for Erica

Erica is 11 years old and has been diagnosed with severe intellectual disabilities. She communicates with others through single-word statements but has good receptive language. Erica has a strong supportive family and is attending a regular fifth-grade class with the assistance of peer tutors, a part-time instructional assistant, and a special education teacher who contributes time on curriculum adaptations. A major strength of Erica's school program is the strong social relationships she has developed with typical peers. One problem, however, is that during assignments when Erica is supposed to be working on her own, she engages in loud noises (talk outs) and will leave her seat and interact with other students. The teacher perceives this behavior as very disruptive for the class. The teacher's assessment is that the problem behaviors are maintained by

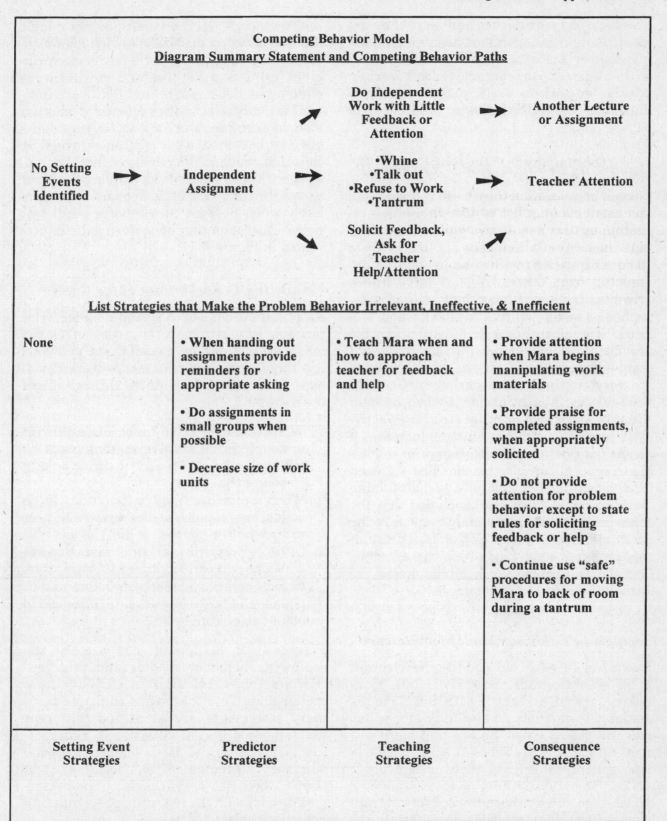

Figure 3.8 Competing Behavior Model and Intervention Strategies for Mara

access to peer attention and that they are most likely if independent assignments are given after Erica has gone for long periods without direct peer contact. Erica's teacher, special education staff, and mother produced the competing behavior plan shown in Figure 3.9.

Competing Behavior Model for Cornell

Cornell is a real sweetheart. He is 6 years old and carries a long list of disability labels including autism and severe/profound intellectual disability. Cornell does not use words to speak and varies in what he appears to understand from others. He has large brown eyes that melt your heart, but he also is described as being "willful," "difficult," and "isolated." Cornell spends a significant part of his day sitting and tapping (hitting) his right temple with his right wrist. The movements are very rhythmic and consistent. Cornell's head-hitting is most common when he is in situations in which no other structured activity is occurring. His head-hitting increases if he has not taken his medication prior to coming to school. Cornell's teacher has searched for different factors that may be maintaining his head-hitting and has concluded that the behavior is maintained simply because of the automatic effects it creates; that is, it presumably produces some kind of positive effect for Cornell. The competing behavior model for Cornell is presented in Figure 3.10.

Competing Behavior Model for Stewart

Stewart is 12 years old and the "heartthrob" of his seventh-grade class. He is tall, good-looking, verbal, and getting B's and C's in his classes. Stewart has no disability labels, but over the past 3 years, he has had more and more difficulty with fights at school. He has been getting into fights about once every 2 weeks. He seriously hurt another student 2 months ago and has been treated for cuts and bruises himself on multiple occasions. Stewart is not in special education, but he is a major concern for the faculty at his middle school. Based on discussions with his teachers, Stewart's verbal reports to the vice principal following fights, and preliminary observations, it appears that fights are initiated when Stewart takes offense at another student's comments or actions. Stewart delivers a verbal threat that is often returned by the other student. Physical conflict then ensues, with both students identifying the other as "starting it." This cycle appears to be more likely when Stewart also reports conflict at home. His competing behavior model is presented in Figure 3.11.

Competing Behavior Model for Curtis

As a final example of the competing behavior process, let's return to the case of Curtis whom we met earlier. Recall that the following three summary statements were developed for Curtis and validated through direct observation:

1. When Curtis is asked to complete difficult or nonpreferred math or reading tasks, he will yell obscenities and/or throw objects to escape the tasks.
2. When a peer has a toy or item that Curtis wants, he will pinch and/or scratch the peer to force him or her to give him the toy.
3. During group work or other situations in which he is receiving little attention, Curtis will call out a teacher's name and/or pound and slap his desk to attempt to obtain attention.

Figures 3.12, 3.13, and 3.14 present the competing behavior models and intervention strategies relevant to each of these statements. Note that when multiple summary statements are identified (different functions in different situations), a competing behavior model is developed for *each* summary statement. The overall plan of support becomes a synthesis of the strategies developed from the multiple competing behavior models.

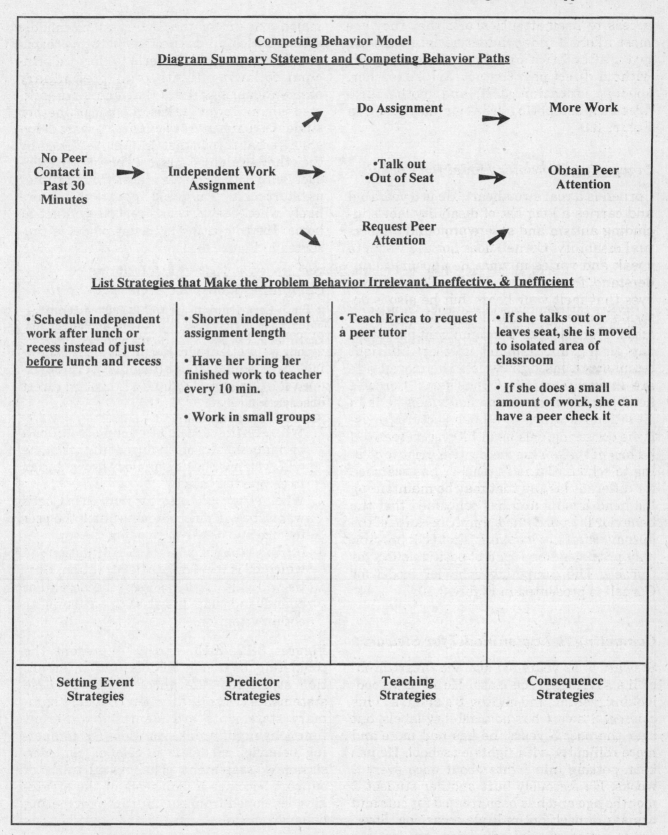

Figure 3.9 Competing Behavior Model and Intervention Strategies for Erica

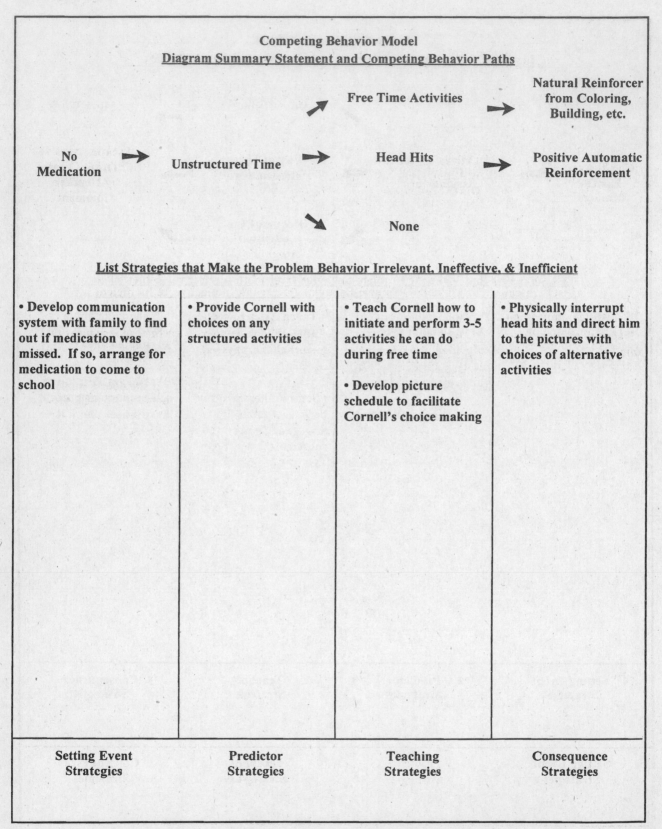

Figure 3.10 Competing Behavior Model and Intervention Strategies for Cornell

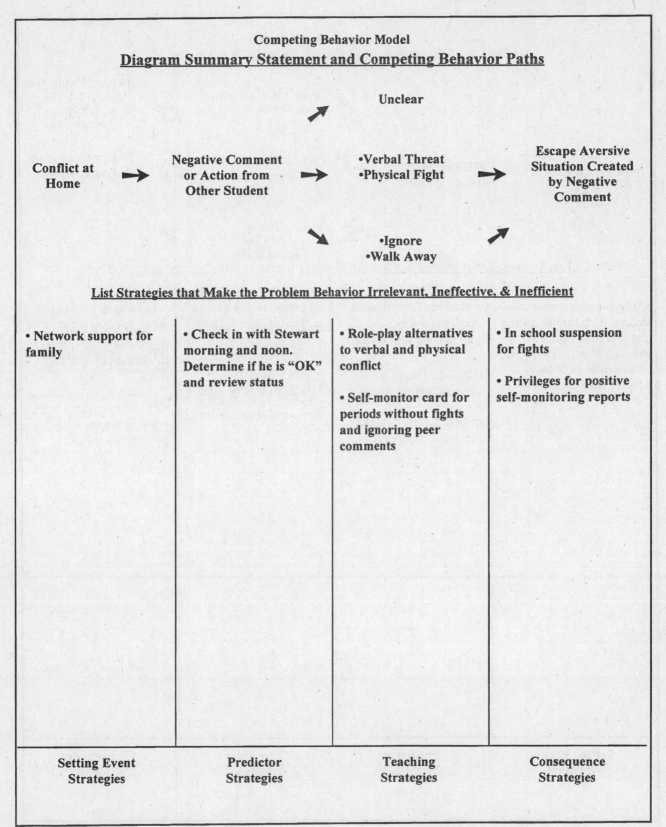

Figure 3.11 Competing Behavior Model and Intervention Strategies for Stewart

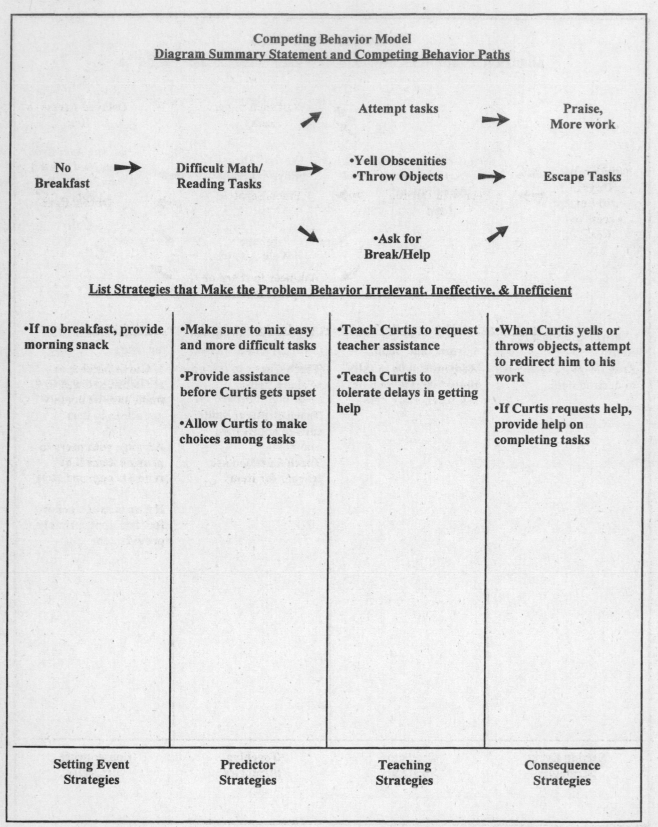

Figure 3.12 Competing Behavior Model for Curtis: Yelling and Throwing

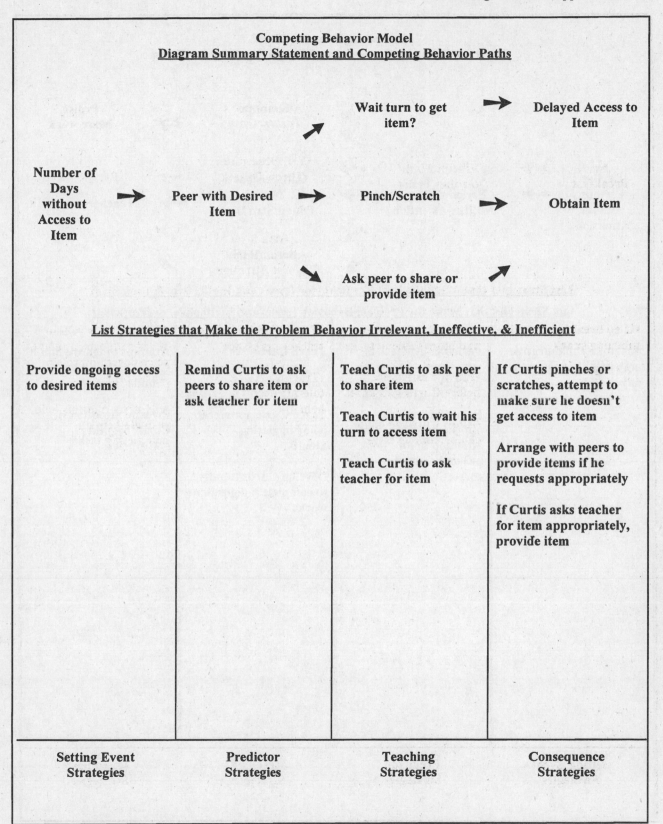

Figure 3.13 Competing Behavior Model for Curtis: Pinching and Scratching

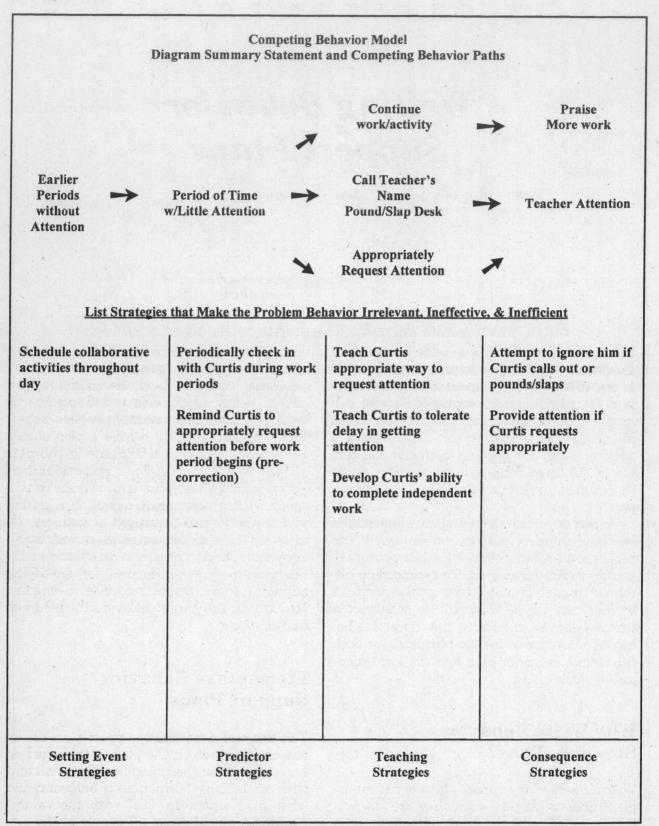

Figure 3.14 Competing Behavior Model for Curtis: Calling Out, Slapping, and Pounding

CHAPTER FOUR

Writing Behavior Support Plans

Behavior support plans are the professional documents that define what we expect to do in our effort to change the likelihood of undesirable behavior in a person and how we will monitor our effectiveness. Most states, school districts, and support organizations have a specific form for writing behavior support plans. All these forms can be useful and can be adapted to define effective plans of support.

In our approach to behavioral support, the behavior support plan becomes simply the professional description of the competing behavior model strategies. The competing behavior model is used like a blueprint. A builder can use a blueprint to construct a complete house. Similarly, the competing behavior model provides the blueprint for both the formal behavior plan and the implementation of that plan.

Why Write Behavior Support Plans?

Written behavior support plans serve multiple functions. At one level, they are the professional documents that demonstrate a coherent, rational plan of support. They are part of our legal, administrative, and professional standards for quality.

On a different level, behavior support plans are formats for clearly defining exactly what will be done to reduce problem behaviors. The assumptions behind a plan should be defined, and all participants in the plan should read it and see their responsibilities. An effective written plan improves the consistency with which multiple staff in a setting will implement the proposed procedures. An effective written plan provides a clear strategy for monitoring progress. An effective written plan provides a format for modifying support procedures in response to ongoing changes in the target individual's behavior and context.

Elements of Behavior Support Plans

The heart of a behavior support plan lies in the extent to which the plan is (a) based on functional assessment results, (b) consistent with fundamental principles of behavior, and (c) a good contextual "fit" with the values, resources, and skills of all people in the setting. The plan's effectiveness is determined by the extent to which (a) it results in change in the behavior of the staff/family and (b) changes in the behavior of staff/family result in change in the behavior of the person receiving support. We have found many formats for behavior plans to be equally useful. Regardless of the format, however, a good behavior support plan should include the following key features:

1. Operational description of the problem behaviors
2. Summary statements resulting from a functional assessment
3. General approach for making problem behaviors irrelevant, inefficient, and ineffective
   a. Setting event strategies
   b. Immediate predictor strategies
   c. Instructional interventions (what will be taught)
   d. Consequence interventions (consequences for maintaining desired and alternative behaviors and reducing problem behaviors)
4. Specific descriptions of (a) typical routines and (b) most difficult problem situations
5. Monitoring and evaluation plan

Operational Descriptions

A behavior support plan should include clear descriptions of problem behaviors. These descriptions should follow traditional behavioral convention. They should be clear enough that a person reading the plan can identify instances and noninstances of each problem behavior.

Summary Statements

Behavior support plans should include the summary statements derived from the functional assessment. This is the element of behavior plans most often neglected. Our experience has shown that agreement on the summary statements increases consistency in plan implementation and that recording the summary statements in the behavior support plan helps ensure that all procedural elements of the plan are conceptually consistent with the information obtained from the functional assessment. In some cases, summary statements may simply be provided in written form. In other cases, it may be helpful to provide the competing behavior model diagram. In several cases, staff have simply attached the competing behavior model form (see Figure 3.7 and Appendix G) to the behavior support description.

Although many options are available, the key feature is to ensure that the summary statements and the hypotheses they contain are an overt part of the behavior support plan.

General Approach

The general approach section of the behavior support plan is a description of the intervention procedures developed through the competing behavior model. The overall goal is to identify a set of procedures that make problem behaviors irrelevant, inefficient, and ineffective. In most cases, this section of the plan will include at least four subsections: (a) setting event strategies, (b) immediate predictor strategies, (c) teaching strategies, and (d) consequence strategies. The section should clearly define what the staff/family will do to reduce the problem behaviors.

Key Routines

No behavior support plan can contain a detailed description of every possible interaction or event. In many cases, however, it is important and helpful to include scripted descriptions of the daily routines that are most common and the problem situations that are most difficult.

An effective behavior support plan describes in detail how to respond when the most dangerous and difficult behaviors occur. Although every effort will be made to develop proactive procedures that decrease the likelihood of problem behaviors, family and staff should assume that any problem behaviors observed in an individual in the past will occur in the future. A behavior support plan that does not have clearly defined procedures for responding to these difficult situations is incomplete.

Monitoring and Evaluation

Behavior support plans should receive ongoing evaluation. The two key questions for any plan are these: (a) Is the plan having any impact on the behavior of the staff, family, and others in the target setting? and (b) Is the plan having any impact on the behavior of the target person? Historically, we measure the behavior of the target person and infer that the plan is influencing the behavior of staff/family.

The section of the behavior support plan that defines monitoring and evaluation procedures should indicate (a) the system that will be used for collecting data and (b) the process for data review (how often and by whom). An example would be to use the Functional Assessment Observation form (FAO) for data collection, to have the staff of the classroom review the data each morning, and to have a formal review of the data with the teacher and behavior consultant during a brief meeting once a week. Weekly summaries of the data would be sent home with the student, and monthly or quarterly meetings with key individual education plan (IEP) team members would be scheduled.

Behavior support plans not only come in many formats; they also come in many lengths. Complex plans addressing life-threatening behaviors may be many pages long. Other plans may be as short as one or two pages. The length of plans can be dictated by a number of factors, only some of which are related to producing effective behavior change. Longer plans are not necessarily more effective or more desirable.

Example Behavior Support Plan: Mara

Earlier in the handbook we described a situation in which an 8-year-old girl named Mara was having difficulty in her second-grade class. Mara carried no disability labels but was engaging in more and more tantrums in her second-grade classroom. Her teacher had requested that Mara be assessed and potentially moved to a classroom that would be more appropriate for her. A functional assessment interview and observation resulted in the competing behavior model in Figure 3.8. From the competing behavior model, her teacher and behavior specialist identified the intervention strategies listed in Figure 3.8. A written behavior support plan for this intervention is presented in Figure 4.1.

BEHAVIOR SUPPORT PLAN FOR MARA

Problem Behaviors

1. *Whining:* Making a high-pitched noise or inflection with negative intonation
2. *Talking out:* Talking during independent seat work without permission of the teacher
3. *Refusing to work:* Not orienting toward or progressing on assigned tasks
4. *Having a tantrum:* Screaming, hitting, biting, and kicking others; destroying property; throwing materials

Functional Assessment Summary Statements

When given independent seat work and 5–10 minutes without teacher or peer attention, Mara will whine, talk out, refuse to work, and/or have a tantrum. These behaviors are maintained by access to teacher attention, even though the teacher has clearly shown that she does not want Mara to engage in these problem behaviors. No clear setting events were identified. A competing behavior model was used to organize the support plan.

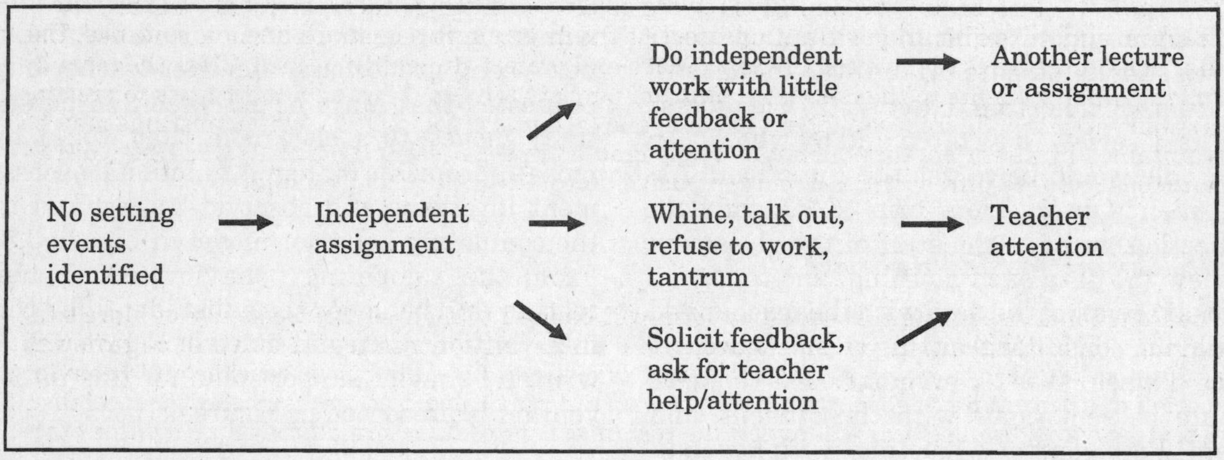

General Approach

Setting event strategies: None.

Predictor strategies: Specific procedures include these: (a) Precorrect Mara when handing out work so she practices the procedures for asking for teacher attention. (b) Change Mara's independent work assignments so she has several small sets of work to complete with the instruction to bring completed sets to the teacher. (Note there is no indication that the work is too difficult for Mara so there is no need to change the content of the assignments.) (c) Consider options for doing assignments in small groups, which may make access to teacher attention irrelevant.

Teaching strategies: Conduct a 10-minute training session with Mara on (a) how the shorter assignments are indicated on her materials, (b) how to request teacher help (hand raise), and (c) how to approach the teacher when she completes a segment of the assignment.

Consequence strategies:
1. The teacher will acknowledge Mara when she first begins independent work assignments.
2. If Mara completes a segment of work and brings it to the teacher, the teacher will stop, praise her for the work she has completed, and confirm the next segment to be completed.

(continued)

Figure 4.1 Example Behavior Support Plan for Mara

3. If Mara engages in whining, talk outs, or refusals, the teacher will ignore the behavior or ask "What is the right way to get help?" or "What is the right way to tell me you have finished?"
4. If Mara engages in tantrums the teacher will continue to use the school-approved "Safe" program to protect Mara from injuring herself, or other students. If Mara's behavior places other children at risk, the teacher will move all other students to the hall and request assistance from the office.

Routines

Independent math assignments: Math assignments typically have 30 problems to be completed. Draw a solid line after the 10th and 20th problems. When you pass out the assignment, instruct Mara to bring you her assignment after she completes the first 10 problems and ask her to show you how she will request your help if she needs it (such as raising her hand). As you hand out the remainder of the independent assignments, note whether Mara begins to work and acknowledge that she (and others) have started.

When she completes problems and brings them to you, praise her for working (do not correct the problems at that time), acknowledge that she is making good progress, and review how many more problems she needs to do before coming back.

Tantrum: If Mara begins screaming, throwing objects, or hitting others, direct her to the rear of the room and isolate her from other students. Use the intercom to request assistance, if needed. Use the "Safe" procedures to physically redirect Mara and protect students if needed. Clear the room by moving other students to the hall if the tantrum persists. The goal during a tantrum is to prevent (a) injury to Mara, (b) injury to other students, and (c) damage to property. While tantrums may be maintained by attention, they cannot be safely ignored in the present context. At this time, Mara's tantrums are very infrequent and more intrusive procedures are not warranted.

Monitoring and Evaluation

The Functional Assessment Observation form will be used to monitor the frequency of Mara's (a) whining, (b) talking out, (c) refusing to work, and (d) having tantrums. The data will be reviewed by the teacher each morning prior to the start of class and weekly by the teacher and behavior specialist to determine whether changes in the plan are warranted. The teacher, behavior specialist, parent, and an administrator will review the results of the program formally within 3 months of its implementation.

Figure 4.1 *(continued)*

Conclusion

Children and adults with problem behaviors will become more active members of our society and contribute more only if we become more competent at designing environments and providing support that prevents, replaces, and reduces those behaviors. We are better equipped to meet this challenge today than we have ever been before. We have a better understanding of the etiology of problem behaviors than we have had in the past. We also have a bettter understanding of how to use behavioral principles to the advantage of both persons with problem behaviors *and* all others around them.

Functional assessment is a key to effective behavioral support. In many ways, functional assessment links the values and the technology associated with behavioral support. Many research studies have documented the value of functional assessment procedures, and many texts have defined the behavioral procedures found to be effective. This handbook is targeted at bringing together advances in assessment with advances in support and intervention strategies.

To develop your familiarity and fluency, use the tools in this handbook—the Functional Assessment Interview (FAI), Student-FAI, Functional Assessment Observation form (FAO), and Competing Behavior Model—at least three times. The first time you will feel awkward and the process may be time-consuming. The second time you will find the process faster and less difficult. By the third time you will be developing fluency and perhaps will have found adaptations that make the tools a better fit for your situations. After you have used the tools and procedures three times, ask whether you are (a) more likely to conduct a functional assessment, (b) more efficient at conducting a functional assessment, (c) more informed after conducting a functional assessment, and (d) better able to transfer functional assessment information into effective behavior support plans. If the answers you provide are affirmative, then keep using the tools that work for you.

We have great respect for behavior analysis as a theory and applied behavior analysis as a technology. We hope the material in this handbook will assist teachers, clinicians, and families to design and implement effective behavioral support—support that results not only in reduced levels of problem behaviors for individuals but also in increased opportunities and improved quality of life.

APPENDIX A

List of References Relevant to Functional Assessment

References and Resources Related to Positive Behavioral Support Approaches

Carr, E. G., & Carlson, J. I. (1993). Reduction of severe behavior problems in the community using multi-component treatment approaches: Extension into community settings. *Journal of Applied Behavior Analysis, 26,* 157–172.

Carr, E. G., Levin, L., McConnachie, G., Carlson, J. I., Kemp, D. C., & Smith, C. (1993). Communication-based treatment of severe behavior problems. In R. Van Houten & S. Axelrod (Eds.), *Behavior analysis and treatment* (pp. 231–267). New York: Plenum.

Carr, E. G., Levin, L., McConnachie, G., Carlson, J. I., Kemp, D. C. & Smith, C. E. (1994). *Communication-based intervention for problem behavior: A user's guide for producing positive change.* Baltimore: Paul H. Brookes.

Carr, E. G., Robinson, S., & Palumbo, L. W. (1990). The wrong issue: Aversive vs. nonaversive treatment. The right issue: Functional vs. nonfunctional treatment. In A. C. Repp & N. N. Singh (Eds.), *Perspectives on the use of nonaversive and aversive interventions for persons with developmental disabilities* (pp. 361–379). Pacific Grove, CA: Brooks/Cole.

Cataldo, M. F., & Harris, J. (1982). The biological basis for self-injury in the mentally retarded. *Analysis and Intervention in Developmental Disabilities, 2,* 21–39.

Catania, A. C. (1992). *Learning* (3rd ed.). Englewood Cliffs, NJ: Prentice Hall.

Donnellan, A. M., LaVigna, G. W., Zambito, J., & Thvedt, J. (1985). A time-limited intensive intervention program model to support community placement for persons with severe behavior problems. *Journal of the Association for Persons with Severe Handicaps, 10,* 123–131.

Donnellan, A. M., LaVigna, G. W., Negri-Shoultz, N., & Fassbender, L. L. (1988). *Progress without punishment: Effective approaches for learners with severe behavior problems.* New York: Teachers College Press.

Durand, V. M. (1990). *Severe behavior problems: A functional communication training approach.* New York: Guilford.

Durand, V. M., & Kishi, G. (1987). Reducing severe behavior problems among persons with dual sensory impairments: An evaluation of a technical assistance model. *Journal of the Association for Persons with Severe Handicaps, 12,* 2–10.

Dyer, K., Dunlap, G., & Winterling, V. (1990). The effects of choice-making on the serious problem behaviors of students with developmental disabilities. *Journal of Applied Behavior Analysis, 23,* 515–524.

Favell, J. E., McGimsey, J. F., & Schell, R. M. (1982). Treatment of self-injury by providing alternate sensory activities. *Analysis and Intervention in Developmental Disabilities, 2,* 83–104.

Foster-Johnson, L., Ferro, J., & Dunlap, G. (1994). Preferred curricular activities and reduced problem behaviors in students with intellectual disabilities. *Journal of Applied Behavior Analysis, 27,* 493–504.

Helmstetter, E., & Durand, V. M. (1991). Nonaversive interventions for severe behavior problems. In L. H. Meyer, C. A. Peck, & L. Brown (Eds.), *Critical issues in the lives of people with severe disabilities* (pp. 559–600). Baltimore: Paul H. Brookes.

Horner, R. H., Albin, R. W., & O'Neill, R. E. (1991). Supporting students with severe intellectual disabilities and severe challenging behaviors. In G. Stoner, M. R. Shinn, & H. M. Walker (Eds.), *Interventions for achievement and behavior problems* (pp. 269–287). Washington, DC: National Association of School Psychologists.

Horner, R. H., & Carr, E. G. (1996). *Behavioral support for students with severe disabilities: Functional assessment and comprehensive intervention.* Manuscript submitted for publication.

Horner, R. H., Close, D. W., Fredericks, H. D., O'Neill, R. E., Albin, R. W., Sprague, J. R., Kennedy, C. H., Flannery, K. B., & Tuesday-Heathfield, L. (1996). Supported living for people with profound disabilities and severe problem behaviors. In D. H. Lehr & F. Brown (Eds.), *People with disabilities who challenge the system* (pp. 209–240). Baltimore: Paul H. Brookes.

Horner, R. H., Dunlap, G., Koegel, R. L., Carr, E. G., Sailor, W., Anderson, J., Albin, R. W., & O'Neill, R. E. (1990). Toward a technology of "nonaversive" behavioral support. *Journal of the Association for Persons with Severe Handicaps, 15*(3), 125–132.

Kincaid, D. (1996). Person-centered planning. In Koegel, L. K., Koegel, R. L., & Dunlap, G. (Eds.), *Positive behavioral support: Including people with difficult behavior in the community* (pp. 439–465). Baltimore: Paul H. Brookes.

Koegel, L. K., Koegel, R. L., & Dunlap, G. (1996). *Positive behavioral support: Including people with difficult behavior in the community.* Baltimore: Paul H. Brookes.

Koegel, L. K., Koegel, R. L., Hurley, C., & Frea, W. D. (1992). Improving social skills and disruptive behavior in children with autism through self-management. *Journal of Applied Behavior Analysis, 25*(2), 341–353.

LaVigna, G. W., & Donnellan, A. M. (1986). *Alternatives to punishment: Solving behavior problems with nonaversive strategies.* New York: Irvington.

LaVigna, G. W., Willis, T. J., & Donnellan, A. M. (1989). The role of positive programming in behavioral treatment. In E. Cipani (Ed.), *The treatment of severe behavior disorders: Behavior analysis approaches* (pp. 59–83). Washington, DC: American Association on Mental Retardation.

Lucyshyn, J. M., & Albin, R. W. (1993). Comprehensive support to families of children with disabilities and behavior problems: Keeping it "friendly." In G. H. S. Singer & L. E. Powers (Eds.), *Families, disability, and empowerment: Active coping skills and strategies for family interventions* (pp. 365–407). Baltimore: Paul H. Brookes.

Lucyshyn, J. M., Nixon, C. D., Glang, A., & Cooley, E. (in press). Comprehensive family support for behavioral change in children with traumatic brain injury. In G. H. S. Singer, A. Glang, & J. Williams (Eds.), *Families and children with acquired brain injury: Challenges and adaptation.* Baltimore: Paul H. Brookes.

Lucyshyn, J. M., Olson, D., & Horner, R. H. (1995). Building an ecology of support: A case study of one young woman with severe problem behaviors living in the community. *Journal of the Association for Persons with Severe Handicaps, 20,* 16–30.

Meyer, L. H., & Evans, I. M. (1989). *Nonaversive intervention for behavior problems: A manual for home and community.* Baltimore: Paul H. Brookes.

Mount, B. (1991). *Person-centered planning: A sourcebook of values, ideals and method to encourage person-centered development.* New York: Graphic Futures.

National Institutes of Health. (1989, September). *Treatment of destructive behaviors.* Rockville, MD: Abstracts presented at NIH Consensus Development Conference.

Newton, J. S., Ard, W. R., & Horner, R. H. (1993). Validating predicted activity preferences of individuals with severe disabilities. *Journal of Applied Behavior Analysis, 26,* 239–245.

Nyhan, W. L., Johnson, H. G., Kaufman, I. A., & Jones, K. L. (1980). Serotonergic approaches to the modification of behavior in the Lesch-Nyhan syndrome. *Applied Research in Mental Retardation, 1,* 25–40.

O'Brien, J., Mount, B., & O'Brien, C. (1991). *Framework for accomplishment: Personal profile.* Decatur, GA: Responsive Systems Associates.

Reichle, J., & Wacker, D. P. (1993). *Communicative alternatives to challenging behavior: Integrating functional assessment and intervention strategies.* Baltimore: Paul H. Brookes.

Risley, T. (1996). Get a life! Positive behavioral intervention for challenging behavior through life arrangement and life coaching. In L. K. Koegel, R. L. Koegel, & G. Dunlap (Eds.), *Positive behavioral support: Including people with difficult behavior in the community* (pp. 425–437). Baltimore: Paul H. Brookes.

Vandercook, T., York, J., & Forest, M. (1989). The McGill Action Planning System (MAPS): A strategy for building the vision. *Journal of the Association for Persons with Severe Handicaps, 14,* 202–215.

Van Houten, R., Axelrod, S., Bailey, J. S., Favell, J. E., Foxx, R. M., Iwata, B. A., & Lovaas, O. I. (1988). The right to effective behavioral treatment. *The Behavior Analyst, 11,* 111–114.

Wolery, M., Bailey, D. B., & Sugai G. M. (1988). *Effective teaching: Principles and procedures of applied behavior analysis with exceptional students.* Boston: Allyn & Bacon.

References and Resources Related to Functional Assessment and Program Development Processes

Albin, R. W., Horner, R. H., & O'Neill, R. E. (1994). *Proactive behavioral support: Structuring environments.* Eugene: Specialized Training Program, University of Oregon.

Albin, R. W., Lucyshyn, J. M., Horner, R. H., & Flannery, K. B. (1996). Contextual fit for behavioral support plans: A model for "goodness-of-fit." In L. K. Koegel, R. L. Koegel, & G. Dunlap (Eds.), *Positive behavioral support: Including people with difficult behavior in the community* (pp. 81–98). Baltimore: Paul H. Brookes.

Arndorfer, R. E., Miltenberger, R. E., Woster, S. H., Rortvedt, A. K., & Gaffeney, T. (1994). Home-based descriptive and experimental analysis of problem behaviors in children. *Topics in Early Childhood Special Education, 14,* 64–87.

Axelrod, S. (1987). Functional and structural analysis of behavior: Approaches leading to reduced use of punishment procedures. *Research in Developmental Disabilities, 8,* 165–178.

Bailey, J. S., & Pyles, D. A. M. (1989). Behavioral diagnostics. In E. Cipani (Ed.), *The treatment of severe behavior disorders: Behavior analysis approaches* (pp. 85–107). Washington, DC: American Association on Mental Retardation.

Bijou, S. W., Peterson, R. F., & Ault, M. H. (1968). A method to integrate descriptive and experimental field studies at the level of data and empirical concepts. *Journal of Applied Behavior Analysis, 1,* 175–191.

Carr, E. G. (1988). Functional equivalence as a mechanism of response generalization. In R. H. Horner, G. Dunlap, & R. L. Koegel (Eds.), *Generalization and maintenance: Lifestyle changes in applied settings* (pp. 221–241). Baltimore: Paul H. Brookes.

Carr, E. G., & Durand, V. M. (1985). Reducing behavior problems through functional communication training. *Journal of Applied Behavior Analysis, 18,* 111–126.

Carr, E. G., Langdon, N. A., & Yarbrough, S. (in press). Hypothesis-based intervention for severe problem behavior. In A. C. Repp & R. H. Horner (Eds.), *Functional analysis of problem behavior: From effective assessment to effective support.* Pacific Grove, CA: Brooks/Cole.

Carr, E. G., Reeve, C. E., & Magito-McLaughlin, D. (1996). Contextual influences on problem behavior in people with developmental disabilities. In L. K. Koegel, R. L. Koegel, & G. Dunlap (Eds.), *Positive behavioral support: Including people with difficult behavior in the community* (pp. 403–423). Baltimore: Paul H. Brookes.

Cooper, L. J., & Harding, J. (1993). Extending functional analysis procedures to outpatient and classroom settings for children with mild disabilities. In J. Reichle & D. P. Wacker (Eds.), *Communicative alternatives to challenging behavior: Integrating functional assessments and intervention strategies* (pp. 41–62). Baltimore: Paul H. Brookes.

Day, H. M., Horner, R. H., & O'Neill, R. E. (1994). Multiple functions of problem behaviors: Assessment and intervention. *Journal of Applied Behavior Analysis, 27,* 279–289.

Day, R. M., Rea, J. A., Schussler, N. G., Larsen, S. E., & Johnson, W. L. (1988). A functionally based approach to the treatment of self-injurious behavior. *Behavior Modification, 12,* 565–589.

Derby, K. M., Wacker, D. P., Peck, S., Sasso, G., DeRaad, A., Berg, W., Asmus, J., & Ulrich, S. (1994). Functional analysis of separate topographies of aberrant behavior. *Journal of Applied Behavior Analysis, 27,* 267–278.

Derby, K. M., Wacker, D. P., Sasso, G., Steege, M., Northup, J., Cigrand, K., & Asmus, J. (1992). Brief functional assessment techniques to evaluate aberrant behavior in an outpatient setting: A summary of 79 cases. *Journal of Applied Behavior Analysis, 25,* 713–721.

Donnellan, A. M., Mirenda, P. L., Mesaros, R. A., & Fassbender, L. L. (1984). Analyzing the communicative functions of aberrant behavior. *Journal of the Association for Persons with Severe Handicaps, 9,* 201–212.

Dunlap, G., & Kern, L. (1993). Assessment and intervention for children within the instructional curriculum. In J. Reichle & D. Wacker (Eds.), *Communicative approaches to the management of challenging behavior* (pp. 177–203). Baltimore: Paul H. Brookes.

Dunlap, G., Kern-Dunlap, L., Clarke, S., & Robbins, F. R. (1991). Functional assessment, curricular revision, and severe behavior problems. *Journal of Applied Behavior Analysis, 24,* 387–397.

Dunlap, G., Kern, L., dePerczel, M., Clarke, S., Wilson, D., Childs, K. E., White, R., & Falk, G. D. (1993). Functional analysis of classroom variables for students with emotional and behavioral challenges. *Behavioral Disorders, 18,* 275–291.

Durand, V. M. (1988). The motivation assessment scale. In M. Hersen & A. S. Bellack (Eds.), *Dictionary of behavioral assessment techniques.* New York: Pergamon Press.

Durand, V. M., & Carr, E. G. (1987). Social influences on "self-stimulatory" behavior: Analysis and treatment application. *Journal of Applied Behavior Analysis, 20,* 119–132.

Durand, V. M., & Carr, E. G. (1988). Identifying the variables maintaining self-injurious behavior. *Journal of Autism and Developmental Disorders, 18,* 99–117.

Durand, V. M., & Crimmins, D. B. (1988). Identifying the variables maintaining self-injurious behavior. *Journal of Autism and Developmental Disorders, 18,* 99–117.

Durand, V. M., & Crimmins, D. B. (1988). *The motivation assessment scale: An administration manual.* Unpublished manuscript. Albany: State University of New York at Albany.

Farber, J. (1987). Psychopharmacology of self-injurious behavior in the mentally retarded. *Journal of the American Academy of Child & Adolescent Psychiatry, 26,* 296–302.

Flannery, B. K., O'Neill, R. E., & Horner, R. H. (1995). Including predictability in functional assessment and individual program development. *Education and Treatment for Children, 18(4),* 499–509.

Foster-Johnson, L., & Dunlap, G. (1993). Using functional assessment to develop effective, individualized interventions for challenging behaviors. *Teaching Exceptional Children, 25,* 44–50.

Foster-Johnson, L., Ferro, J., & Dunlap, G. (1994). *Curricular Activity Profile.* Tampa: Florida Mental Health Institute, University of South Florida.

Foster-Johnson, L., Ferro, J., & Dunlap, G. (1994). *Curriculum: An introduction to community-referenced curricula.* FMHI Publication Series No. CFS 140. Tampa: Florida Mental Health Institute, University of South Florida.

Frea, W. D., Koegel, L. K., & Koegel, R. L. (1993). *Understanding why problem behaviors occur: A guide for assisting parents in assessing causes of behavior and designing treatment plans.* Santa Barbara: University of California.

Groden, G. (1989). A guide for conducting a comprehensive behavioral analysis of a target behavior. *Journal of Behavior Therapy and Experimental Psychiatry, 20,* 163–169.

Gunsett, R. P., Mulick, J. A., Fernald, W. B., & Martin, J. L. (1989). Indications for medical screening prior to behavioral programming for severely and profoundly mentally retarded clients. *Journal of Autism and Developmental Disorders, 19,* 167–172.

Halle, J. W., & Spradlin, J. E. (1993). Identifying stimulus control of challenging behavior: Extending the analysis. In J. Reichle & D. P. Wacker (Eds.), *Communicative alternatives to challenging behavior: Integrating functional assessments and intervention strategies* (pp. 83–109). Baltimore: Paul H. Brookes.

Haring, T. G., & Kennedy, C. H. (1990). Contextual control of problem behavior in students with severe disabilities. *Journal of Applied Behavior Analysis, 23,* 235–243.

Horner, R. H., & Billingsley, F. F. (1988). The effect of competing behavior on the generalization and maintenance of adaptive behavior in applied settings. In R. H. Horner, G. Dunlap, & R. L. Koegel (Eds.), *Generalization and maintenance: Lifestyle changes in applied settings* (pp. 197–220). Baltimore: Paul H. Brookes.

Horner, R. H., O'Neill, R. E., & Flannery, K. B. (1993). Building effective behavior support plans from functional assessment information. In M. Snell (Ed.), *Instruction of persons with severe handicaps* (4th ed., pp. 184–214). Columbus, OH: Merrill.

Horner, R. H., Vaughn, B., Day, H. M., & Ard, B. (1996). The relationship between setting events and problem behavior. In L. K. Koegel, R. L. Koegel, & G. Dunlap (Eds.), *Positive behavioral support: Including people with difficult behavior in the community* (pp. 381–402). Baltimore: Paul H. Brookes.

Iwata, B. A., Dorsey, M. F., Slifer, K. J., Bauman, K. E., & Richman, G. S. (1982). Toward a functional analysis of self-injury. *Analysis and Intervention in Developmental Disabilities, 2,* 3–20. Reprinted in *Journal of Applied Behavior Analysis,* 1994, *27,* 197–209.

Iwata, B. A., Pace, G. M., Dorsey, M. F., Zarcone, J. R., Vollmer, T. R., Smith, R. G., Rodgers, T. A., Lerman, D. C., Shore, B. A., Mazakski, J. L., Goh, H. L., Cowdery, G. E., Kalsher, M. J., McCosh, K. C., & Willis, K. D. (1994). The functions of self-injurious behavior: An experimental epidemiological analysis. *Journal of Applied Behavior Analysis, 27,* 215–240.

Iwata, B. A., Pace, G. M., Kalsher, M. J., Cowdery, G. E., & Cataldo, M. F. (1990). Experimental analysis and extinction of self-injurious escape behavior. *Journal of Applied Behavior Analysis, 23,* 11–27.

Iwata, B. A., Vollmer, T. R., & Zarcone, J. R. (1990). The experimental (functional) analysis of behavior disorders: Methodology, applications, and limitations. In A. C. Repp & N. N. Singh (Eds.), *Perspectives on the use of nonaversive and aversive interventions for persons with developmental disabilities* (pp. 301–330). Pacific Grove, CA: Brooks/Cole.

Kanfer, F. H., & Saslow, G. (1969). Behavioral diagnosis. In C. M. Franks (Ed.), *Behavior therapy: Appraisal and status* (pp. 417–444). New York: McGraw-Hill.

Kemp, D., & Carr, E. G. (in press). Reduction of severe problem behavior in community employment using an hypothesis-driven multicomponent intervention approach. *Journal of the Association for Persons with Severe Handicaps.*

Kennedy, C. H., Horner, R. H., & Newton, J. S. (1990). The social networks and activity patterns of adults with severe disabilities: A correlational analysis. *Journal of the Association for Persons with Severe Handicaps, 15*(2), 86–90.

Kennedy, C. H., Horner, R. H., Newton, J. S., & Kanda, E. (1990). Measuring the activity patterns of adults with severe disabilities living in the community. *Journal of the Association for Persons with Severe Handicaps, 15*(2), 79–85.

Kern, L., Childs, K. E., Dunlap, G., Clarke, S., & Falk, G. D. (1994). Using assessment-based curricular intervention to improve the classroom behavior of a student with emotional and behavioral challenges. *Journal of Applied Behavior Analysis, 27,* 7–19.

Kern, L., & Dunlap, G. (in press). Assessment-based interventions for children with emotional and behavioral disorders. In A. C. Repp & R. H. Horner (Eds.), *Functional analysis of problem behavior: From effective assessment to effective support.* Pacific Grove, CA: Brooks/Cole.

Kern, L., Dunlap, G., Clarke, S., & Childs, K. E. (1994). Student-assisted functional assessment interview. *Diagnostique, 19,* 29–39.

Lalli, J. S., & Goh, H. L. (1993). Naturalistic observations in community settings. In J. Reichle & D. P. Wacker (Eds.), *Communicative alternatives to challenging behavior: Integrating functional assessment and intervention strategies* (pp. 11–39). Baltimore: Paul H. Brookes.

Lennox, D. B., & Miltenberger, R. G. (1989). Conducting a functional assessment of problem behavior in applied settings. *Journal of the Association for Persons with Severe Handicaps, 14,* 304–311.

Mace, F. C., & Lalli, J. S. (1991). Linking descriptive and experimental analyses in the treatment of bizarre speech. *Journal of Applied Behavior Analysis, 24,* 553–562.

Mace, F. C., Page, T. J., Ivancic, M. T., & O'Brien, S. (1986). Analysis of environmental determinants of aggression and disruption in mentally retarded children. *Applied Research in Mental Retardation, 7,* 203–221.

Munk, D. D., & Repp, A. C. (1994). Behavioral assessment of feeding problems of individuals with severe disabilities. *Journal of Applied Behavior Analysis, 27,* 241–250.

Myrianthopoulos, N. C. (1981). Gilles de la Tourette syndrome. In P. J. Vinken & G. W. Bruyn (Eds.), *Handbook of clinical neurology, 42,* 221–222. Amsterdam: North Holland.

Northup, J., Wacker, D., Sasso, G., Steege, M., Cigrand, K., Cook, J., & DeRaad, A. (1991). A brief functional analysis of aggressive and alternative behavior in an out-clinic setting. *Journal of Applied Behavior Analysis, 24,* 509–522.

Nyhan, W. L. (1981). Lesch-Nyhan syndrome. In P. J. Vinken & G. Bruyn (Eds.), *Handbook of clinical neurology, 42,* 152–154. Amsterdam: North Holland.

O'Neill, R. E., Horner, R. H., O'Brien, M., & Huckstep, S. (1991). Generalized reduction of difficult behaviors: Analysis and intervention in a competing behaviors framework. *Journal of Developmental and Physical Disabilities, 3*(1), 5–20.

Pyles, D. A. M., & Bailey, J. S. (1990). Diagnosing severe behavior problems. In A. C. Repp & N. N. Singh (Eds.), *Perspectives on the use of nonaversive and aversive interventions for persons with developmental disabilities* (pp. 382–401). Pacific Grove, CA: Brooks/Cole.

Repp, A. C., Felce, D., & Barton, L. E. (1988). Basing the treatment of stereotypic and self-injurious behaviors on hypotheses of their causes. *Journal of Applied Behavior Analysis, 21,* 281–289.

Singh, N. N., & Pulman, R. M. (1979). Self-injury in the de Lange Syndrome. *Journal of Mental Deficiency Research, 23,* 79–84.

Sprague, J. R., & Horner, R. H. (1992). Covariation within functional response classes: Implications for treatment of severe problem behavior. *Journal of Applied Behavior Analysis, 25,* 735–745.

Sprague, J. S., & Horner, R. H. (1995). Functional assessment and intervention in community settings. *Mental Retardation and Developmental Disabilities Research Reviews, 1,* 89–93.

Sprague, J. S., & Horner, R. H. (in press). Low frequency, high intensity problem behavior: Toward an applied technology of functional assessment and intervention. In A. C. Repp & R. H. Horner (Eds.), *Functional analysis of problem behavior: From effective assessment to effective support.* Pacific Grove, CA: Brooks/Cole.

Steege, M. W., Wacker, D. P., Berg, W. K., Cigrand, K. K., & Cooper, L. J. (1989). The use of behavioral assessment to prescribe and evaluate treatments for severely handicapped children. *Journal of Applied Behavior Analysis, 22,* 23–33.

Sturmey, P., Carlsen, A., Crisp, A. G., & Newton, J. T. (1988). A functional analysis of multiple aberrant responses: A refinement and extension of Iwata et al.'s (1982) methodology. *Journal of Mental Deficiency Research, 32,* 31–49.

Touchette, P. E., MacDonald, R. F., & Langer, S. N. (1985). A scatter plot for identifying stimulus control of problem behavior. *Journal of Applied Behavior Analysis, 18,* 343–351.

Tuesday-Heathfield, L., O'Neill, R., Horner, R. H., Ezzell, J., & Ouellette, L. (1992). *The role of multiple functions in behavioral intervention.* Unpublished manuscript.

Vollmer, T. R., Marcus, B. A., Ringdahl, J. E., & Roane, H. S. (1995). Progressing from brief assessments to extended experimental analyses in the evaluation of aberrant behavior. *Journal of Applied Behavior Analysis, 28,* 561–576.

Wacker, D., Steege, M., Northup, J., Reimers, T., Berg, W., & Sasso, G. (1990). Use of functional analysis and acceptability measures to assess and treat severe behavior problems: An outpatient model. In A. C. Repp & N. N. Singh (Eds.), *Perspectives on the use of nonaversive and aversive interventions for persons with developmental disabilities* (pp. 349–359). Pacific Grove, CA: Brooks/Cole.

Wahler, R. G., & Fox, J. J. (1981). Setting events in applied behavior analysis: Toward a conceptual and methodological expansion. *Journal of Applied Behavior Analysis, 14,* 327–338.

APPENDIX B

Functional Assessment Interview Form (FAI)

FUNCTIONAL ASSESSMENT INTERVIEW (FAI)

Person of concern _____ Age _____ Sex M F

Date of interview _____ Interviewer _____

Respondents _____

A. DESCRIBE THE BEHAVIORS.

1. For each of the behaviors of concern, define the topography (how it is performed), frequency (how often it occurs per day, week, or month), duration (how long it lasts when it occurs), and intensity (how damaging or destructive the behaviors are when they occur).

	Behavior	Topography	Frequency	Duration	Intensity
a.					
b.					
c.					
d.					
e.					
f.					
g.					
h.					
i.					
j.					

2. Which of the behaviors described above are likely to occur together in some way? Do they occur about the same time? In some kind of predictable sequence or "chain"? In response to the same type of situation?

_____

_____

1

B. DEFINE ECOLOGICAL EVENTS (SETTING EVENTS) THAT PREDICT OR SET UP THE PROBLEM BEHAVIORS.

1. What *medications* is the person taking (if any), and how do you believe these may affect his or her behavior?

_____

_____

_____

2. What *medical* or *physical conditions (if any)* does the person experience that may affect his or her behavior (e.g., asthma, allergies, rashes, sinus infections, seizures, problems related to menstruation)?

_____

_____

_____

3. Describe the *sleep patterns* of the individual and the extent to which these patterns may affect his or her behavior.

_____

_____

_____

4. Describe the *eating routines and diet* of the person and the extent to which these may affect his or her behavior.

_____

_____

_____

5a. Briefly list below the person's typical daily schedule of activities. (Check the boxes by those activities the person enjoys and those activities most associated with problems.)

Enjoys	Problems			Enjoys	Problems		
☐	☐	6:00	_____	☐	☐	2:00	_____
☐	☐	7:00	_____	☐	☐	3:00	_____
☐	☐	8:00	_____	☐	☐	4:00	_____
☐	☐	9:00	_____	☐	☐	5:00	_____
☐	☐	10:00	_____	☐	☐	6:00	_____
☐	☐	11:00	_____	☐	☐	7:00	_____
☐	☐	12:00	_____	☐	☐	8:00	_____
☐	☐	1:00	_____	☐	☐	9:00	_____

5b. To what extent are the activities on the daily schedule *predictable* for the person, with regard to what will be happening, when it will occur, with whom, and for how long?

_____

_____

_____

5c. To what extent does the person have the opportunity during the day to *make choices* about his or her activities and reinforcing events? (e.g., food, clothing, social companions, leisure activities)

_____

_____

_____

6. How many other persons are typically around the individual at home, school, or work (including staff, classmates, and housemates)? Does the person typically seem bothered in situations that are more *crowded and noisy?*

_____

_____

_____

7. What is the pattern of *staffing support* that the person receives in home, school, work, and other settings (e.g., 1:1, 2:1)? Do you believe that the *number* of staff, the *training* of staff, or their *social interactions with the person* affect the problem behaviors?

_____

_____

_____

C. DEFINE SPECIFIC IMMEDIATE ANTECEDENT EVENTS THAT PREDICT WHEN THE BEHAVIORS ARE *LIKELY* AND *NOT LIKELY* TO OCCUR.

1. *Times of Day: When* are the behaviors most and least likely to happen?

Most likely: _____

_____

Least likely: _____

_____

3

2. *Settings:* *Where* are the behaviors most and least likely to happen?

   Most likely: _____

   _____

   Least likely: _____

   _____

3. *People:* *With whom* are the behaviors most and least likely to happen?

   Most likely: _____

   _____

   Least likely: _____

   _____

4. *Activity:* *What activities* are most and least likely to produce the behaviors?

   Most likely: _____

   _____

   Least likely: _____

   _____

5. Are there particular or idiosyncratic situations or events not listed above that sometimes seem to "set off" the behaviors, such as particular demands, noises, lights, clothing?

   _____

   _____

6. What *one thing* could you do that would most likely make the undesirable behaviors occur?

   _____

   _____

7. Briefly describe how the person's behavior would be affected if . . .
   a. You asked him or her to perform a difficult task.

   _____

   _____

   b. You interrupted a desired activity, such as eating ice cream or watching TV.

   _____

   _____

   c. You unexpectedly changed his or her typical routine or schedule of activities.

   _____

   _____

d. She or he wanted something but wasn't able to get it (e.g., a food item up on a shelf).

_____

_____

e. You didn't pay attention to the person or left her or him alone for a while (e.g., 15 minutes).

_____

_____

D. IDENTIFY THE CONSEQUENCES OR OUTCOMES OF THE PROBLEM BEHAVIORS THAT MAY BE MAINTAINING THEM (I.E., THE FUNCTIONS THEY SERVE FOR THE PERSON IN PARTICULAR SITUATIONS).

1. Think of each of the behaviors listed in Section A, and try to identify the *specific* consequences or outcomes the person gets when the behaviors occur in different situations.

Behavior	*Particular situations*	*What exactly does he or she get?*	*What exactly does she or he avoid?*

a. _____

b. _____

c. _____

d. _____

e. _____

f. _____

g. _____

h. _____

i. _____

j. _____

E. CONSIDER THE OVERALL *EFFICIENCY* OF THE PROBLEM BEHAVIORS. EFFICIENCY IS THE COMBINED RESULT OF (A) HOW MUCH *PHYSICAL EFFORT* IS REQUIRED, (B) *HOW OFTEN* THE BEHAVIOR IS PERFORMED BEFORE IT IS REWARDED, AND (C) *HOW LONG* THE PERSON MUST WAIT TO GET THE REWARD.

	Low Efficiency				High Efficiency
_____	1	2	3	4	5
_____	1	2	3	4	5
_____	1	2	3	4	5
_____	1	2	3	4	5
_____	1	2	3	4	5

F. WHAT *FUNCTIONAL ALTERNATIVE* BEHAVIORS DOES THE PERSON ALREADY KNOW HOW TO DO?

1. What socially appropriate behaviors or skills can the person already perform that may generate the same outcomes or reinforcers produced by the problem behaviors?

_____

_____

_____

G. WHAT ARE THE PRIMARY WAYS THE PERSON COMMUNICATES WITH OTHER PEOPLE?

1. What are the general expressive communication strategies used by or available to the person? These might include vocal speech, signs/gestures, communication boards/books, or electronic devices. How consistently are the strategies used?

_____

_____

_____

2. On the following chart, indicate the behaviors the person uses to achieve the communicative outcomes listed:

Communicative Functions	Complex speech (sentences)	Multiple-word phrases	One-word utterances	Echolalia	Other vocalizing	Complex signing	Single signs	Pointing	Leading	Shakes head	Grabs/reaches	Gives objects	Increased movement	Moves close to you	Moves away or leaves	Fixed gaze	Facial expression	Aggression	Self-injury	Other
Request attention																				
Request help																				
Request preferred food/objects/activities																				
Request break																				
Show you something or some place																				
Indicate physical pain (headache, illness)																				
Indicate confusion or unhappiness																				
Protest or reject a situation or activity																				

3. With regard to the person's receptive communication, or ability to understand other persons . . .

   a. Does the person follow spoken requests or instructions? If so, approximately how many? (List if only a few.)

   _____

   _____

   b. Does the person respond to signed or gestural requests or instructions? If so, approximately how many? (List if only a few.)

   _____

   _____

   c. Is the person able to imitate if you provide physical models for various tasks or activities? (List if only a few.)

   _____

   _____

   d. How does the person typically indicate *yes or no* when asked if she or he wants something, wants to go somewhere, and so on?

   _____

   _____

H. WHAT ARE THINGS YOU *SHOULD DO* AND THINGS YOU *SHOULD AVOID* IN WORKING WITH AND SUPPORTING THIS PERSON?

   1. What things can you do to improve the likelihood that a teaching session or other activity will go well with this person?

   _____

   _____

   _____

   2. What things should you avoid that might interfere with or disrupt a teaching session or activity with this person?

   _____

   _____

   _____

I. WHAT ARE THINGS THE PERSON LIKES AND ARE REINFORCING FOR HIM OR HER?

   1. *Food items:* _____

   _____

7

2. *Toys and objects:* _____

_____

_____

3. *Activities at home:* _____

_____

_____

4. *Activities / outings in the community:* _____

_____

_____

5. *Other:* _____

_____

_____

J. WHAT DO YOU KNOW ABOUT THE HISTORY OF THE UNDESIRABLE BEHAVIORS, THE PROGRAMS THAT HAVE BEEN ATTEMPTED TO DECREASE OR ELIMINATE THEM, AND THE EFFECTS OF THOSE PROGRAMS?

Behavior	*How long has this been a problem?*	*Programs*	*Effects*
1.			
2.			
3.			
4.			
5.			
6.			
7.			
8.			
9.			
10.			

K. DEVELOP SUMMARY STATEMENTS FOR EACH MAJOR PREDICTOR AND/OR CONSEQUENCE.

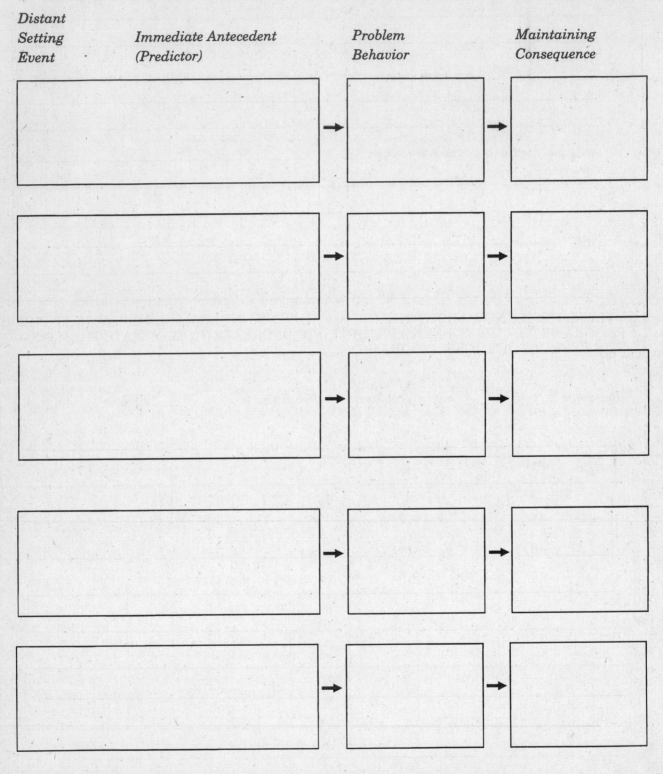

Distant
Setting
Event

Immediate Antecedent
(Predictor)

Problem
Behavior

Maintaining
Consequence

9

APPENDIX C

Student-Directed Functional Assessment Interview Form

Student-Directed Functional Assessment Interview

Student Name: _____   Interviewer: _____

Referring Teacher: _____   Date: _____

I. Opening. *"We are meeting today to find ways to change school so that you like it more. This interview will take about 30 minutes. I can help you best if you answer honestly. You will not be asked anything that might get you in trouble."*

Assist the student to identify specific behaviors that are resulting in problems in the school or classroom. Making suggestions or paraphrasing statements can help the student clarify his or her ideas. You should have a list of behaviors nominated by the referring teacher.

II. Define the behaviors of concern. * *"What are the things you do that get you in trouble or are a problem?"* *(Prompts: Late to class? Talk out in class? Don't get work done? Fighting?)*

Behavior   Comment

1.

2.

3.

4.

5.

III. Complete student schedule. *Use the "Student Daily Schedule" matrix to identify the times and classes in which the student performs problem behavior. Focus the interview on those times that are **most likely** to result in problem behavior.*

* You will use the numbers to the left as codes for the identified behaviors as you complete the rest of the interview.

1

Student Daily Schedule

Please place an "X" in each column to show the times and classes where you have difficulty with the behaviors we talked about. If you have a lot of difficulty during a period, place an "X" on or near the 6. If you have a little difficulty during the class or hall time, place the "X" on or near the 1. We can practice on a couple together before we start.

Subject, Teacher	Before School	1st Period	Hall	2nd Period	Hall	3rd Period	Hall	4th Period	Lunch	5th Period	Hall	6th Period	Hall	7th Period	Hall	8th Period	After School
Most Difficult 6																	
5																	
4																	
3																	
2																	
Least Difficult 1																	

2

Summary Statement Form

Place/Activity/Event	Predictor	Problem Behavior(s)	Maintaining Consequences

④ → ② → ① → ③

Complete the summary statement diagram following the numbered sequence (Behavior(s) first, then Predictors, etc.). Consider the items below as possible elements for inclusion in the summary statement. Complete a **different** summary statement for each new consequence.

④ What Important Events, Places, or Activities Tend to be Associated with the Behavior?

Lack of sleep _____
Illness _____
Physical pain _____
Hunger _____
Trouble at home _____
Fight/conflict with Peers _____
Noise/distractions _____
Activity/Class _____
Other _____

② What Appears to Set off Problem Behavior

Class demands that are:
  -too hard _____
  -boring _____
  -unclear _____
  -long _____
Teacher reprimands _____
Peer teasing _____
Peer encouragement _____
Other _____

① What do the Problem Behaviors Look Like?

Late to class _____
Talk out in class _____
Disruptions _____
Inappropriate language _____
Disrespectful behavior _____
Property destruction _____
Carrying weapons _____
Fidget _____
Not completing work _____
Steal _____
Threaten _____
Vandalism _____
Insubordination _____
Other _____

③ What Does the Student Gain From the Problem Behaviors?

Escape or Avoid
  -teacher demands _____
  -teacher reprimands _____
  -teacher correction _____
  -peer social contact _____
    (teasing)
  -tasks (hard, long) _____

Get Attention
  -from peers _____
  -from teacher/adult _____

Get Activity or Item
  -access to game _____
  -access to toy _____
  -access to food _____
  -access to money _____
  -access to task _____

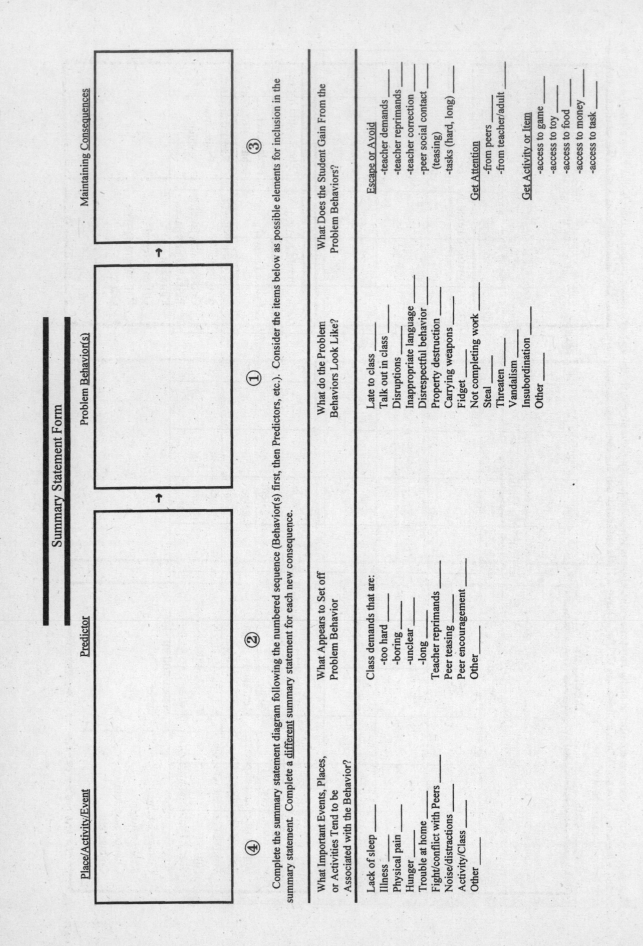

3

Building a Support Plan

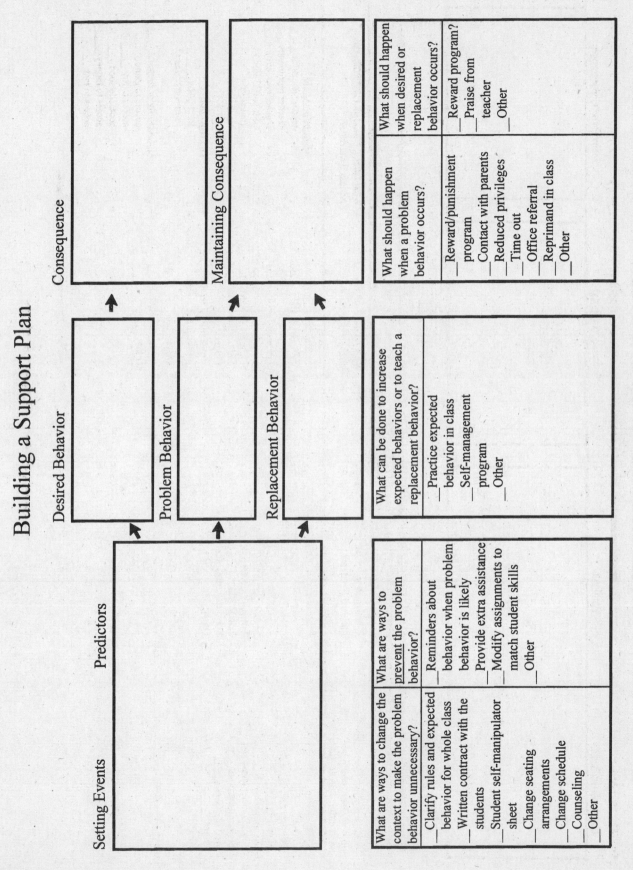

Setting Events

Predictors

Desired Behavior

Consequence

Problem Behavior

Replacement Behavior

Maintaining Consequence

What are ways to change the context to make the problem behavior unnecessary?

___ Clarify rules and expected behavior for whole class
___ Written contract with the students
___ Student self-manipulator sheet
___ Change seating arrangements
___ Change schedule
___ Counseling
___ Other

What are ways to <u>prevent</u> the problem behavior?

___ Reminders about behavior when problem behavior is likely
___ Provide extra assistance
___ Modify assignments to match student skills
___ Other

What can be done to increase expected behaviors or to teach a replacement behavior?

___ Practice expected behavior in class
___ Self-management program
___ Other

What should happen when a problem behavior occurs?

___ Reward/punishment program
___ Contact with parents
___ Reduced privileges
___ Time out
___ Office referral
___ Reprimand in class
___ Other

What should happen when desired or replacement behavior occurs?

___ Reward program?
___ Praise from teacher
___ Other

4

APPENDIX D

Blank Functional Assessment Observation Form

Functional Assessment Observation Form

Name:

Starting Date:

Ending Date:

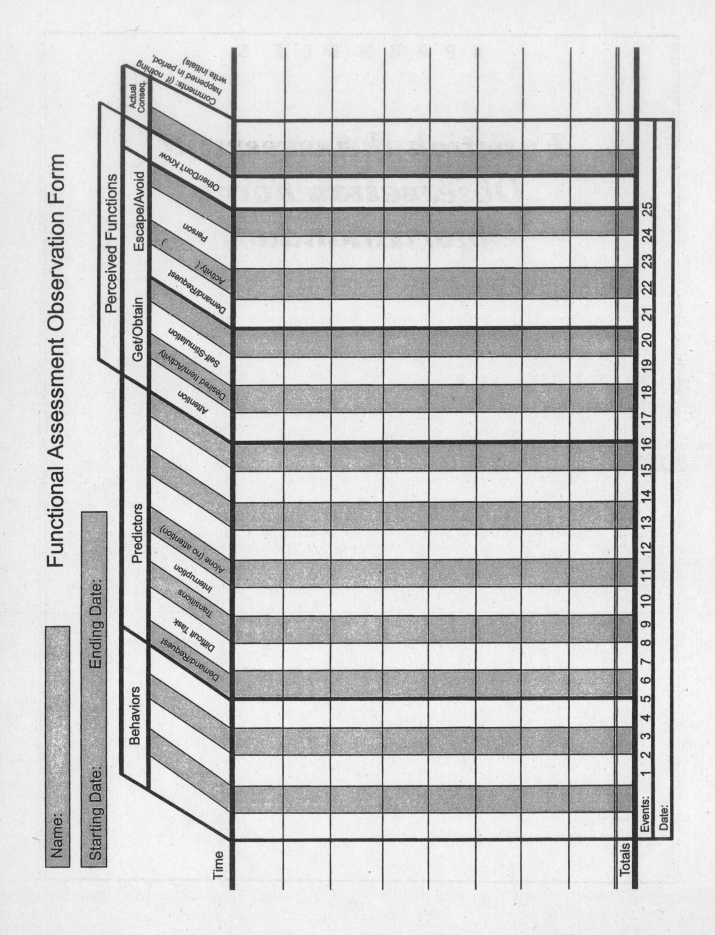

APPENDIX E

Functional Assessment Observation Form for Yolanda

Functional Assessment Observation Form

Name: *Yolanda M.*

Starting Date: *1/30/96*   Ending Date: *2/1/96*

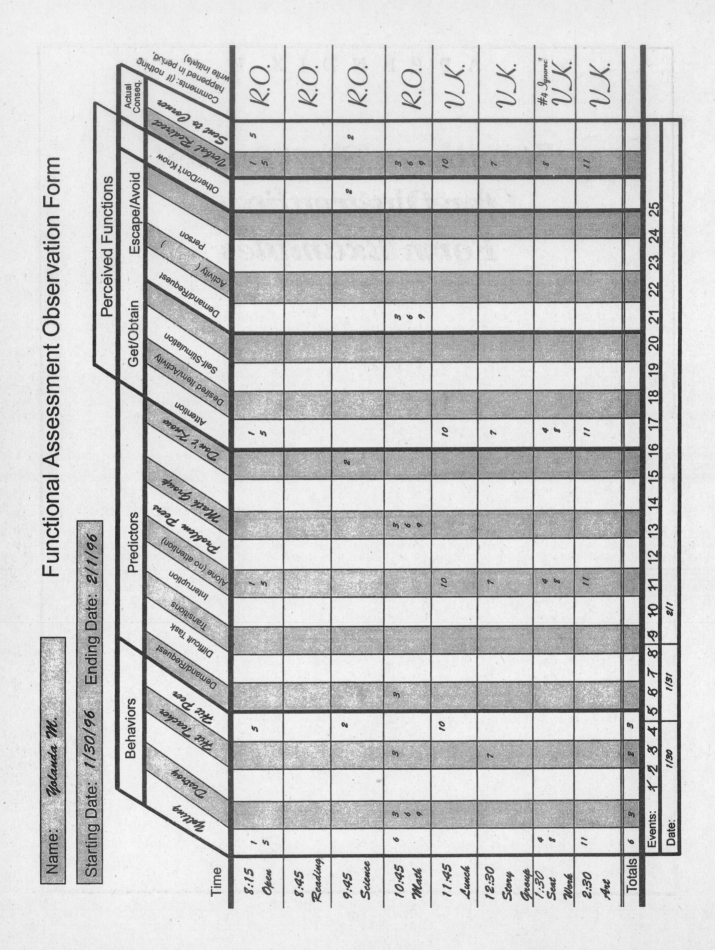

Time	Behaviors				Predictors							Perceived Functions							Actual Conseq.	Comments
	Yelling	Destroy	Hit Teacher	Hit Peer	Demand/Request	Difficult Task	Transitions	Interruption	Alone (no attention)	Problem Peer	Math Group	Don't Know	Attention	Desired Item/Activity	Self-Stimulation	Demand/Request	Activity ( )	person ( )	Other/Don't Know	Sent to Corner / Verbal Redirect	
8:15 Open	1 5		5					5				1 5	1 5							5 / 1 5	R.O.
8:45 Reading																				R.O.
9:45 Science	6 9	3 6 9	3	2		3	2				2	2								2 /	R.O.
10:45 Math	6									3 6 9					3 6 9				/ 3 6 9	R.O.
11:45 Lunch				10				10				10	10							/ 10	V.K.
12:30 Story Group			7					7				7	7							/ 7	V.K.
1:30 Seat Work	4 8							4 8				4 8	4 8							/ 8	#4 Ignored V.K.
2:30 Art	11							11				11	11							/ 11	V.K.
Totals	6 9		2 3																	

Events:	1 2 3	4 5 6 7	8 9	10 11 12	13 14 15	16 17	18 19 20	21 22 23 24 25
Date:	1/30	1/31	2/1					

A P P E N D I X   F

Summary Statements for Observation Form Examples

Erin

Statement 1: When Erin is asked to do nonpreferred tasks at work, she will begin dropping and breaking objects to escape from the task demands.

Peter

Statement 1: When Peter is asked to complete shaving and other self-care routines, he will bite his wrist and grab or push staff members to escape from those activities.

Statement 2: When Peter is not receiving attention or interaction, he will bite his wrist and hit his face to obtain such attention and interaction.

Curtis

Statement 1: When Curtis is asked to complete difficult math or nonpreferred math or reading tasks, he will yell obscenities and/or throw objects to escape from the tasks. (Note: FAOF does not provide information about distant setting events.)

Statement 2: When a peer has a toy or item that Curtis wants, he will pinch and/or scratch the peer to get the child to give him the toy or item.

Statement 3: During group work or other situations in which he is receiving little attention, Curtis will call out a teacher's name and/or pound and slap his desk to attempt to obtain attention.

Note: Arm scratching was not observed, so related summary statements were not supported (based on these limited data). Should be followed up with teachers.

A P P E N D I X G

Blank Competing
Behavior Model Form

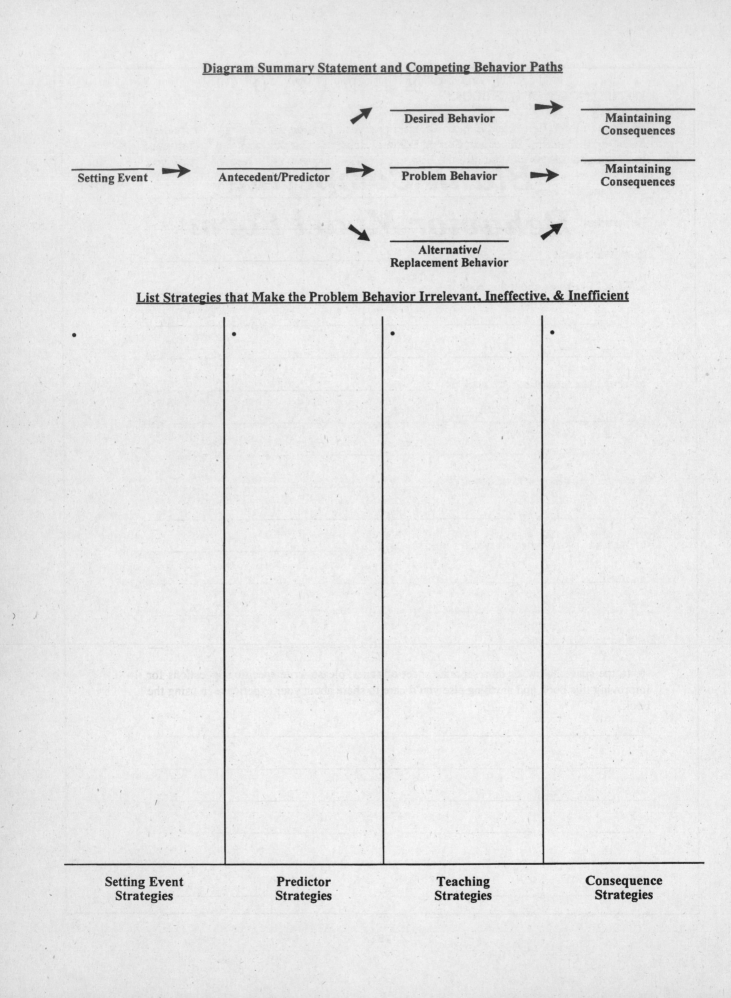

Diagram Summary Statement and Competing Behavior Paths

Desired Behavior → Maintaining Consequences

Setting Event → Antecedent/Predictor → Problem Behavior → Maintaining Consequences

Alternative/ Replacement Behavior

List Strategies that Make the Problem Behavior Irrelevant, Ineffective, & Inefficient

Setting Event Strategies	Predictor Strategies	Teaching Strategies	Consequence Strategies
•	•	•	•

TO THE OWNER OF THIS BOOK:

We hope that you have found *Functional Assessment and Program Development for Problem Behavior: A Practical Handbook*, Second Edition, useful. So that this book can be improved in a future edition, would you take the time to complete this sheet and return it? Thank you.

School and address: _____

Department: _____

Instructor's name: _____

1. What I like most about this book is: _____

_____

_____

2. What I like least about this book is: _____

_____

_____

3. My general reaction to this book is: _____

_____

4. The name of the course in which I used this book is: _____

_____

5. Were all of the chapters of the book assigned for you to read? _____

   If not, which ones weren't? _____

 6. In the space below, or on a separate sheet of paper, please write specific suggestions for improving this book and anything else you'd care to share about your experience in using the book.

_____

_____

_____

_____

_____

_____

FOLD HERE

BROOKS/COLE
CENGAGE Learning

BUSINESS REPLY MAIL
FIRST-CLASS MAIL   PERMIT NO. 34   BELMONT CA

POSTAGE WILL BE PAID BY ADDRESSEE

Attn: *Robert E. O'Neill et al.*

Brooks/Cole
10 Davis Drive
Belmont, CA 94002-3098

NO POSTAGE
NECESSARY
IF MAILED
IN THE
UNITED STATES

FOLD HERE

OPTIONAL:

Your name: _____   Date: _____

May we quote you, either in promotion for *Functional Assessment and Program Development for Problem Behavior: A Practical Handbook,* Second Edition, or in future publishing ventures?

Yes: _____   No: _____

Sincerely yours,

Robert E. O'Neill
Robert H. Horner
Richard W. Albin
Jeffrey R. Sprague
Keith Storey
J. Stephen Newton